ALLEN CARR'S EASY WAY TO STOP SMOKING

Canadian edition

About the Author

Allen Carr (1934–2006) was a chain smoker for over thirty years. After countless failed attempts to quit, in 1983 he discovered what every smoker dreams about – an easy way to stop smoking. Over the past twenty-five years, Carr has built a network of clinics that spans the globe. Every year, over 50,000 smokers attend his legendary clinics.

Allen Carr's Easy Way to Stop Smoking is one of the biggest selling self-help titles in publishing history. To date, it has already sold around 8 million copies and has topped the bestseller lists in France, Holland, Germany and the UK.

Carr's genius lies in the removal of fear. The Carr method has been successfully adapted for weight control, alcohol control, fear of flying and the teenage smoking problem. For more information and a full list of Carr's titles, please contact any of our clinics, which are listed in the back of this book.

Dedication

To the smokers I have failed to cure,
I hope it will help them to get free.

And to Nancy Toth, who sowed the
acorn in Canada and nurtured the sapling.

Also to Damian O'Hara who will
ensure that Nancy's efforts mature
into a powerful and permanent oak!

But most of all to Joyce.

This edition published for Allen Carr (Canada) by

Clarity Publishing
P.O. Box 61051
511 Maple Grove Rd.
Oakville, ON L6J 6X0

Printed and bound in Canada.

Library and Archives Canada Cataloguing in Publication

Carr, Allen, 1934-2006
Allen Carr's easy way to stop smoking. — Canadian ed.

Includes index.
ISBN 978-0-9734684-0-3

1. Smoking cessation programs. 2. Cigarette habit—Treatment.
3. Self-help techniques. I. Title.

HV5740.C37 2004 613.85 C2004-903865-6

Contents

Preface

At last; a method of stopping smoking that approaches the problem from a smoker's perspective.

If you are looking for a lecture on lung cancer, heart disease etc., then I am sorry to say that this book is not for you. If, however, you are looking for a way to stop smoking that is...

- Easy
- Immediate
- Permanent
- No Withdrawal
- No Willpower
- No Weight Gain
- No tricks or gimmicks

...then all you need to do is read on.

Warning

Perhaps you are somewhat apprehensive about reading this book. Perhaps, like the vast majority of smokers, the mere thought of stopping fills you with panic and although you have every intention of stopping one day, that day is not today.

If you are expecting me to inform you of the terrible health risks that smokers run, that smokers spend a fortune and that you are a weak-willed jellyfish, then I must disappoint you. Those tactics never helped me to quit, and if they were going to help you, they would have done so years ago.

My method, which I shall refer to as EASYWAY doesn't work that way. Some of the things I am about to say you might find difficult to accept. However, by the time you have completed this book, you'll not only believe them, but will wonder how on earth you ever allowed yourself to be brainwashed into believing something different.

There is a common misapprehension that smokers choose to smoke. Smokers no more choose to smoke than alcoholics choose to become alcoholics, or heroin addicts choose to become heroin addicts. It is true that we chose to light those first experimental cigarettes. I occasionally choose to go to see a movie, but I didn't choose to spend the rest of my life sitting in a cinema.

Think about that for a moment. Did you ever make a definite decision that you wouldn't enjoy a meal or a social occasion without a cigarette? Or that you wouldn't be able to relax or handle stress without smoking? At what stage did you decide that you needed cigarettes, not just for social occasions, but that you needed them permanently in your presence, and felt insecure or even panic-stricken without them? Exactly what was the date when you decided that you would be a smoker, puffing away all day, every day, never being able to stop? The average Canadian smoker smoked their first cigarette at age thirteen. Are we really saying that at thirteen we were deciding that we would be a smoker for the rest of our lives?

Like every other smoker on the planet, we fell into a trap. The nicotine trap is the most subtle, sinister trap that man and nature have combined to devise. There is not a parent on this planet, whether they are a smoker or non-smoker that would encourage their kids to smoke. What this really means is that they wish that they themselves had never started. Not surprising really, no one needs cigarettes to enjoy life or cope with stress before they get hooked.

At the same time that all smokers want to quit, all smokers also want to keep smoking. After all, no one forces us to light up. Whether we understand the reason or not, it is only smokers themselves who decide to light up.

If there were a magic button that smokers could press and wake up tomorrow morning as if they had never smoked, the only smokers left smoking would be the youngsters who are still at the experimental stage, convinced they could never get hooked. Didn't we all start that way?

The truth is that the only thing that keeps us smoking, the only thing that prevents us from breaking free, is:

FEAR

Fear that we will have to struggle through the rest of our lives feeling miserable and deprived. Fear that we will have to be armed with endless supplies of willpower to conquer the terrible cravings. Fear that a meal or a social occasion will never be quite as enjoyable without a cigarette. Fear that we'll never be able to concentrate, handle stress or be as confident without our little crutch. Fear that our personality and character will change. Fear that quitting smoking means that our lives will never be as enjoyable. But most of all the fear that you will never truly be free, and that we will spend the rest of our lives wanting to smoke but not being allowed to.

If, as I did, you have already tried all the 'conventional' ways to quit and been through all the misery of the willpower method of stopping, you will not only be dominated by those fears I describe, but also convinced that you can never quit.

If you are apprehensive, panic-stricken or feel that the time is not right for you to quit, then you are being affected by the fear. The fear is not relieved by cigarettes but created by them. Non-smokers don't have any of these fears.

You never decided to fall into the nicotine trap. Like all traps, it is designed to ensure that you remain trapped. Ask yourself, when you lit that first cigarette were you really deciding that you would be a smoker as long as you have been? So when are you going to quit? Tomorrow? New Year's Eve? Weedless Wednesday? Next year? Stop kidding yourself! The trap is designed to hold you for life. Why else do you think all those other smokers don't quit before it kills them?

This book was first published in 1985. It has sold over 7,000,000 copies and been a bestseller every year since then. In Canada over 100,000 copies have been sold since 1996. To put this in context, 5,000 copies is considered a Canadian bestseller. In putting together this updated

Canadian version of the book, I am using twenty years of experience helping smokers in our clinics and eighteen years of feedback from the original book. As you will soon be reading, that feedback has revealed information that has exceeded my wildest dreams of the effectiveness of EASYWAY. It has also revealed two aspects of the method that have caused me concern. The second I will cover later. The first arose out of the many letters I have received from Canadian readers. I give you three typical examples:

> *"I didn't believe the claims you made and I apologize for doubting you. It was just as easy and enjoyable as you said it would be. I've given copies of your book to all my smoking friends and relatives, but I can't understand why they don't read it."*

> *"I was given your book eight years ago by an ex-smoker friend. I've just got around to reading it. My only regret is that I wasted eight years."*

> *"I've just finished reading EASYWAY. I know it has only been four days, but I feel so great. I know I'll never need to smoke again. I first started to read your book five years ago, got halfway through and panicked. I knew that if I went on reading I would have to stop! Wasn't I silly?"*

No, that particular young lady wasn't silly. I've referred to a 'magic button'. EASYWAY works just like that magic button. Let me make it quite clear, EASYWAY isn't magic, but for me and the millions of former smokers who have found it so easy and enjoyable to quit, it seems like magic!

This is the warning. Now we have a chicken and egg situation. Every smoker wants to quit and every smoker can find it easy and enjoyable to do so. It's only fear that prevents smokers from trying to quit. The greatest benefit of quitting is to be rid of that fear. But you won't be free of that fear until you have completed the book. On the contrary, like the lady in the third example; that fear might increase as you are reading and it might prevent you from finishing it.

You didn't decide to fall into this trap. When you were a youngster, you didn't even know the trap existed. You need to be very clear on one point: you will not escape from the trap unless you make a positive decision to do so. You might already be straining at the leash to quit. On the other hand, you might be apprehensive. Either way, please bear in mind: YOU HAVE NOTHING TO LOSE!

If at the end of the book you decide that you wish to continue to smoke, there is nothing to prevent you from doing so. You don't even have to cut down or stop smoking while you are reading the book, and remember, there is no shock treatment. Do you really think that those graphic images on Canadian packs help smokers to quit? If they do, then why are nearly six million Canadians still smoking?

On the contrary, I have nothing but good news for you. Can you imagine how Nelson Mandela must have felt when he was finally released from prison? That's how I felt when I escaped from the nicotine trap. That's how the millions of ex-smokers who have used EASYWAY feel. By the end of the book: THAT'S HOW YOU WILL FEEL!

GO FOR IT!

Introduction

"I'm going to cure the world of smoking."

I was talking to my wife. She thought that I had finally flipped. Understandable if you consider that she had watched me fail on countless occasions. The most recent had been two years previously. I'd actually survived six months of sheer hell before I finally caved in and lit a cigarette. I'm not ashamed to admit that I cried like a baby. I was crying because I knew that I was condemned to be a smoker for the rest of my life. I had put so much effort into that attempt and suffered so much misery that I knew I'd never have the strength to go through that ordeal again. I'm not a violent man, but if some patronizing non-smoker had been stupid enough to suggest to me that all smokers can find it easy to quit, immediately and permanently, I would not have been responsible for my actions. However, I am convinced that any jury in the world, if it comprised only of smokers, would have pardoned me on the grounds of justifiable homicide.

Perhaps you too find it impossible to believe that any smoker can find it easy to quit. If so, I beg you not to toss this book into the nearest garbage can. Please trust me. I assure you that it's true and that any smoker – and that means you too – can find it easy and even enjoyable to quit.

Anyway, there I was, two years later, having just put out what I knew would be my final cigarette, not only telling my wife that I was already a non-smoker, but that I was going to cure the rest of the world too. I must admit, at the time I found her skepticism somewhat irritating. However, in no way did it diminish my feeling of exaltation. I suppose that my exhilaration in knowing that I was already a happy non-smoker distorted my perspective somewhat. With the benefit of hindsight, I can sympathize with her attitude. I now understand why Joyce and my close friends and relatives thought I was a candidate for the funny farm.

As I look back on my life, it almost seems that my whole existence has been a preparation for solving the smoking problem. Even those hateful years of training and practicing as a Chartered Accountant were invaluable in helping me to unravel the mysteries of the smoking trap.

Abe Lincoln once said that you can't fool all the people all the time, but that's exactly what I believe the tobacco companies have been successfully doing for decades. I also believe that I was the first person to really understand the smoking trap. Please don't mistake this statement for arrogance. I wish I could claim that my superior intellect led me to this understanding, but actually it was merely the circumstances of my own life.

The momentous day was July 15th, 1983. I didn't escape from Alcatraz, but it felt like it. Even today, twenty years later, I can remember the feelings of relief, happiness and excitement when I stubbed out that final butt. I realized immediately that I had discovered something that every smoker secretly prayed for: an easy way to stop smoking.

After testing out the method on smoking friends and relatives, I gave up my job as CFO of a large UK company and became a full-time counselor, helping other smokers to get free.

I wrote the first edition of this book in 1985. One of my failures, the man described in Chapter 25, was the inspiration. He visited me twice, and we were both reduced to tears on each occasion. He was so agitated that I couldn't get him to relax enough to listen to what I was saying. I hoped that if I wrote it all down, he could read it in his own good time, as many times as he wanted to, and this would help him absorb the message.

I was in no doubt that EASYWAY would work just as effectively for other smokers as it had for me. However, when I contemplated putting the method into book form, I was apprehensive. I did my own market research. The comments were not very encouraging:

"How can a book help me to quit? What I need is willpower!"

"How can a book help me control the terrible withdrawal pangs?"

In addition to these pessimistic comments, I had my own doubts. Often at the clinics it became obvious that a client had misunderstood an important point that I was making. I was able to correct the situation. But how would a book be able to do that? I remembered well the times when I was studying to be an accountant, when I didn't understand or agree with a certain point, the frustration because you couldn't ask a book to explain. I was also well aware, particularly in this age of the internet, TV and Playstation that many people are no longer accustomed to reading.

Added to all these factors, I had one doubt that overrode the rest. I wasn't a writer and was very conscious of my limitations in this regard. I was confident that I could sit down face-to-face with any smoker and convince them how much more enjoyable social occasions will be, how he or she will be better able to concentrate and handle stress as a non-smoker and just how easy and enjoyable the process of quitting can be. But could I transfer that ability into the written word? I even doubted that I had the right to put EASYWAY into book form and whether I should not have employed a professional writer. In no way was I certain that this would be a success.

Thankfully, I needn't have worried. The gods were kind to me. In the eighteen years since EASYWAY first appeared on the shelves, I have received literally thousands of letters from grateful readers containing comments such as:

'It's the greatest book ever written.'

'You are my guru.'

'You are a genius.'

'You should get a knighthood.'

'You should be Prime Minister.'

'You are a saint.'

It is wonderful and humbling to receive letters such as these, and I hope that I have not let such comments go to my head. I am fully aware that these comments do not allude to my ability as an author, rather they are made despite my limited literary skills. They were made because whether your preference is to read a book or to attend one of our clinics:

The EASYWAY method works!

Not only do we now have a network of over 70 clinics, including locations throughout Canada (for more information visit www.theeasywaytostopsmoking.com or call 1 866 NO NIC 99), but this book now has been translated into over twenty languages. As I write, it is the number one non-fiction bestseller in Germany and has also topped bestseller lists in Holland, France, Spain and the UK. EASYWAY is rarely out of the top 50 bestsellers on Amazon's European websites, and it is also one of their most reviewed books, receiving a five star rating – the highest available. My Norwegian publisher tells me that when the wonderful *Harry Potter and the Order of the Phoenix* was launched, it did not dislodge EASYWAY from the number one spot!

After approximately a year of running clinics, I thought I had learned everything there was to learn about helping smokers to quit. Amazingly, twenty years after uncovering the EASYWAY method, I learn something new practically every day. This fact caused me some concern when I was asked to review the original edition and write this one. I feared that practically everything I had written would need to be amended or retracted.

Again, I needn't have worried. The basic principles of EASYWAY are as sound today as they were when I first committed them to paper. The beautiful truth is: IT IS EASY TO STOP!

That is a fact. My only challenge is to convince smokers that it's true.

At the clinics, we try to achieve perfection. Every single failure hurts us deeply because we know that every smoker can find it easy to quit. When smokers fail, they tend to blame themselves. We regard the failure as ours. We failed to convince those smokers just how easy and enjoyable it is to quit and to stay quit. This is why we offer a money-back guarantee at our clinics. Whilst initially this money-back concept nearly gave my bank manager a heart attack, over the past twenty years his fear was proved to be unfounded as fewer than 5% of clinic attendees make a claim for a refund.

When I started to conduct clinics to help smokers, I originally believed that my biggest enemy would be the tobacco industry. Amazingly, my main stumbling blocks have been the very institutions that I thought would be my greatest allies: the media, the Government and the medical establishment.

I'm a bit of a fan of old movies. I recently watched the marvelous *Sister Kenney*. It's a somewhat obscure film from the 1940s starring Rosalind Russell. It tells the astonishing (and true) story of Sister Elizabeth Kenney, an Australian nurse who worked with children suffering from infantile paralysis, or polio. During the first half of the twentieth century until the discovery of a vaccine in 1954, the word 'polio' caused the same degree of terror as 'cancer' does today. The effect of polio was not only to paralyse the limbs but also to distort them. The established medical treatment of the time was to put the limbs in irons in an attempt to prevent the distortion. The result was paralysis for life.

Sister Kenney rightly believed that the irons inhibited recovery and demonstrated a thousand times over at her clinic that the muscles could be re-trained to enable children to once again walk. However, Sister Kenney was not a doctor. How dare she dabble in an area confined to qualified doctors! It didn't seem to matter that Sister Kenney had found the solution to the problem and had proved her solution to be effective. The children treated by Sister Kenney knew she was right, and so did their parents. Yet the Australian medical establishment not only refused to adopt her methods, but also prevented her from practicing. In 1940 after thirty years of rejection, Sister Kenney moved to the US where she was eventually viewed as a miracle worker. In 1952 she was voted America's Most Admired Woman.

I first saw this movie long before I discovered EASYWAY. It's a wonderful and entertaining story, but surely Hollywood has used a large dollop of poetic license for dramatic effect? Sister Kenney couldn't possibly have discovered something that the medical establishment had failed to? Surely the medical profession weren't the dinosaurs portrayed in the film? How could it possibly take these intelligent, devoted men and women of medicine over twenty years to accept facts that were staring them in the face?

They say that truth is stranger than fiction. I apologize to the makers of *Sister Kenney* for accusing them of using poetic license. I now know first hand the difficulties she faced. Like Sister Kenney, I am just a lone individual without the incredible financial support of the big pharmaceutical companies or of institutions such as ASH or the Non-Smokers Rights Association. Like Sister Kenney, I'm only famous because my method works. Like Sister Kenney, the medical establishment has ignored the experience of thousands upon thousands of people who have found it easy and enjoyable to stop smoking using EASYWAY. Like Sister Kenney, I naively thought that once the establishment had seen the efficacy of my approach they would not hesitate to adopt it. I could not have been more wrong.

You might draw the conclusion that I am no respecter of the medical profession. Nothing could be further from the truth. One of my sons is a doctor and I know of no finer profession. Indeed we receive more referrals to our clinics from doctors than from any other source (apart from referrals from ex-smokers who have attended) and, surprisingly, more of our clients come from the medical profession than from any other.

In the early years I was considered a combination of quack and charlatan. However, in August 1997, I had the great honour to be invited to address the 10th World Conference on Tobacco or Health, hosted by the World Health Organisation in Beijing, China. I believe I am the first person without medical qualifications to be honoured in this way. The invitation itself was a measure of the progress we have made in establishing EASYWAY in the mainstream of the stop smoking methods.

However, I was disappointed to find that my lecture fell on deaf ears. The attendees (mainly doctors and researchers) seemed able only to think in terms of pharmacological approaches to quitting (i.e. treating nicotine addiction by prescribing nicotine). This was fortuitous, as the conference itself was sponsored by the manufacturers of Nicotine Replacement products.

It occurred to me at that conference that almost none of the people in the business of trying to help smokers to quit had ever been smokers themselves. They may have known the molecular structure of nicotine and the impact of continuous exposure to the tars contained in tobacco on the human body, but none of them knew anything about smokers and smoking. More to the point, they knew nothing about quitting.

As a consequence of this gap in their knowledge, the medical establishment's strategy was (and is to this day) to tell smokers what they already know: that they shouldn't smoke because it is disgusting, anti-social, dangerous and expensive. Let's face it, if this strategy worked, there wouldn't be any smokers. Smokers don't smoke for the reasons they shouldn't smoke – every smoker knows that already and if it was going to make them quit, it would have done so years ago.

Even today, the medical profession seems adamant that nicotine replacement products or anti-depressants need to be used when smokers are trying to stop. Whilst we are told that such treatments 'can double your chances' of quitting, the truth is that when all is said and done, such treatments have an 80-95% failure rate (depending on which research you read) but still they are prescribed. How doctors continue to prescribe treatments with such poor levels of success eludes me entirely.

As I write this, the health authorities have just announced the launch of yet another media campaign aimed at discouraging children from starting to smoke by the use of frightening visual images. I recently appeared on TV along with a doctor representing Action on Smoking & Health (ASH), who had never smoked a day in her life and had never cured a single smoker. She categorically informed viewers that this campaign would discourage thousands of children from smoking and thereby save hundreds, or maybe thousands of lives. Sadly, the statistics don't give cause for such optimism. According to the Canadian Tobacco Usage Monitoring Survey (CTUMS), levels of smoking amongst teenagers, particularly teenage girls, has never been higher.

I mention this because it demonstrates the profound lack of understanding that much of the health establishment has of smoking and smokers. So long as teenagers perceive smoking as cool, anti-establishment and a badge of independence and adulthood, they will experiment, irrespective of what the health establishment tells them about the long-term dangers. They know that one cigarette won't kill them, and believe they could never get hooked on something that tastes so disgusting. Isn't that how we all started?

It staggers me that the medical establishment hasn't yet figured out what every parent on the planet knows – that the best way to guarantee that our teenagers start smoking is to tell them not to.

In the original edition of this book I wrote:

'There is a wind of change in society. A snowball has started that I hope this book will help turn into an avalanche.'

Twenty years on and seven million copies later, I think the snowball has grown into the size of a bowling ball, but it is still, to use an eloquent turn of phrase, spit in a bucket. I'm immensely grateful to the thousands of ex-smokers who have attended our clinics, read my books, watched my videos and recommended EASYWAY to their friends, family and colleagues, and I pray that they continue to do so.

It is this word of mouth that will turn the bowling ball into an avalanche. While the medical profession continues to prescribe the latest pill or potion (most of them containing the drug you are trying to kick), more and more smokers will turn to the common sense, painless solution offered by EASYWAY.

The truth, as we have proved countless thousands of times over the years, is that it can be easy and enjoyable to stop smoking. Do you have a feeling of doom and gloom? Forget it. I've been lucky to achieve some wonderful things in my life. By far the greatest was to escape from the slavery of nicotine addiction. I escaped just over twenty years ago and still can't get over the joy of being free. There is no need to feel depressed or miserable. There is nothing bad happening. On the contrary, you are about to achieve what every smoker on the planet would love to achieve: TO BE FREE!

Chapter One

The Worst Nicotine Addict I Ever Met

Perhaps I should begin by describing my qualifications for writing this book. No, I'm not a doctor or psychologist; my qualifications are far more relevant. I spent thirty-three years as a hardcore smoker. In the later years I smoked a hundred a day on a bad day, and never less than sixty.

During my life I had made dozens of attempts to stop. I once stopped for six miserable months. I hated every minute of it, still standing near smokers trying to get a whiff of smoke, still sitting in the smoking compartments of trains (remember when you could still smoke on trains?).

With most smokers it's a case of: 'I'll stop before something happens.' The 'something' was already happening to me. I had reached the stage where I knew it was killing me. I had a permanent headache, which I thought was normal, from the pressure of the constant coughing. I could feel the continuous throbbing of the vein that runs vertically down the centre of my forehead, and I honestly believed that at any moment there would be an explosion in my head and that I would die from a brain hemmorhage. It bothered me and it scared me, but it didn't stop me from smoking.

I had reached the stage where I gave up even trying to stop. It was not so much that I enjoyed smoking. At some stage in their lives most smokers suffer from the illusion that they enjoy some cigarettes, but I didn't. I have always detested the taste and smell, but I thought that a cigarette helped me to relax. It gave me confidence and courage, and I was always miserable when I tried to stop, never being able to visualize an enjoyable life without a cigarette.

During those awful years as a smoker I thought that my life depended on cigarettes, and I was prepared to die rather than be without them. Today, twenty years after I finally broke free from the slavery of smoking, people still ask whether I ever have the odd pang. I truthfully answer: "Never. Never. Never. Just the reverse." I've had a marvelous life. If I had died through smoking, I couldn't have complained. I have been a very lucky man, but the most wonderful thing that has ever happened to me is being freed from that nightmare, the slavery of having to go through life systematically destroying my own body and paying through the nose for the privilege.

Let me make it quite clear from the beginning: I am not a mystical figure. I don't believe in magic or fairies. I have a scientific brain and for quite a while I struggled to understand what had happened to me when I found it so easy to stop. It seemed like magic but it couldn't have been. I started to read books on smoking, hypnosis and psychology. But nothing I read seemed to explain the miracle that had happened. Why had it been so ridiculously easy to stop, whereas previously it had been week after agonizing week of torture and black depression?

It took me a long time to work it all out, basically because I was going about it back-to-front. I was trying to work out why it was so easy to stop, whereas the real questions is 'Why should it be difficult?' Smokers talk about the terrible withdrawal pangs, but when I looked back and tried to remember those awful pangs, they didn't exist for me. There was no physical pain. It was all in the mind.

My full-time job for the last twenty years has been to help other people to stop smoking. I'm very, very successful. Every year around 50,000 smokers attend our clinics. I have personally helped to cure tens of thousands of smokers. Let me emphasize from the start: there is no such thing as a 'confirmed' smoker. I have yet to meet anybody who was as badly hooked (or, rather, *thought* he was as badly hooked) as myself. Anybody can not only stop smoking, but also find it easy to stop. That is a fact. We prove this day-in, day-out at our clinics, which routinely help the hardest of hardcore smokers escape from the smoking trap easily and permanently. It is basically fear that keeps us smoking: the fear that life will never be quite as enjoyable without cigarettes and the fear of feeling deprived. In fact, nothing could be further from the truth. Not only is life just as enjoyable without them but it is infinitely more so. Incredibly, better health and a vastly improved financial position are the least of those gains.

All smokers can find it easy to stop smoking – even you! All you need to do is to read the rest of this book with an open mind. The fact is that if you read this book and follow the instructions, you will find it easy to stop smoking, and enjoyable to stay stopped, just as millions of others have. Most important of all, you won't go through life wanting to smoke or feeling deprived. The only mystery will be why you didn't stop years ago.

Let me issue a warning. There are only two reasons for failure with my method:

1. FAILURE TO CARRY OUT THE INSTRUCTIONS Some people find it annoying that I am so dogmatic about certain recommendations. For example, I will tell you not to try cutting down or using sub-

stitutes like candy, gum etc. (especially substitutes which contain nicotine). The reason I am so dogmatic is because I know my subject. I do not deny that many people have succeeded in stopping using such tools, but they have succeeded despite them, not because of them. There are people who can make love standing on a hammock, but it isn't the easiest way. Everything I tell you has a purpose: to ensure your success by making it easy and enjoyable to stop.

2. FAILURE TO UNDERSTAND Do not take anything for granted. Question not only what I tell you, but also your own preconceptions and attitudes and what society has led you to believe about smoking and quitting. For example, those of you who think that it's just a habit, ask yourself why other habits, some of them enjoyable ones, are easy to break, yet a habit that tastes awful, costs us a fortune and kills us is so difficult to break. Those of you who think you enjoy smoking, ask yourself why you absolutely *have* to smoke that cigarette, but can take or leave other things in life that are infinitely more enjoyable?

Chapter 2

The Easy Way

The aim of this book is to get you into the frame of mind whereby instead of starting with a feeling of doom and gloom and misery and depression, you can start with a feeling of elation, as if you have been cured from a terrible life-threatening disease.

Smokers thinking about quitting are often intimidated by what they perceive to be the scale of the task they face. They feel as if they are attempting to scale Mount Everest single-handed. They believe that they will need to suffer terrible physical withdrawal pangs, that they are giving up their best friend and that they will, in all likelihood, fail anyway. Who could think of a worse frame of mind with which to take on this, or any other project? The smoker has already programmed him or herself to fail. But if you are able to replace those negative thoughts and feelings with an attitude of excitement and anticipation, then the task is made far easier. In fact, with the right frame of mind, it is not only easy, but also incredibly enjoyable to stop smoking. From then on, the further you go through life the more you will look at cigarettes and wonder how you had ever believed that you needed to smoke. You will look at smokers with pity as opposed to envy.

Provided that you are not a non-smoker or an ex-smoker, it is essential to keep smoking until you have finished the book completely. This may appear to be something of a contradiction. Later I shall be explaining that cigarettes do absolutely nothing for you at all. In fact, one of the many puzzles about smoking is that when we are smoking, we look at it and wonder what on earth we're doing. It is only when we can't smoke that we feel that the cigarette is precious or desirable. However, let us accept that, whether you like it or not, you believe you need to smoke and that you can't relax or concentrate properly unless you're smoking. So do not attempt to stop smoking before you have finished the whole book. As you read further, your desire to smoke will gradually fade, until it disappears entirely. Let the book do its work. Remember, all you need to do is to follow the instructions.

With the benefit of eighteen years' feedback since the book's original publication, apart from Chapter 28 (Timing), this instruction to continue to smoke has caused me more frustration than any other. When I first stopped smoking, many of my friends and relatives also stopped, purely because I had done so. They thought, 'If Allen can do it, anyone can.' Over the years, by dropping little hints I managed to persuade the ones that hadn't stopped to realize how nice it is to be free! When the book was first printed I gave copies to the hardcore smokers I knew who were still puffing away. I worked on the basis that even if it was the worst book ever written, they would still read it, if only because it had been written by a friend. I was surprised and hurt to learn that, months later, they hadn't bothered to read it. I even discovered that the original copy I had signed and given to someone who was then my closest friend had not only been ignored but actually given away. I was hurt at the time, but I had overlooked the terrible fear that slavery to the weed instills in the smoker. It can transcend friendship. I nearly provoked a divorce because of it. My mother once said to my wife "Why don't you threaten to leave him if he doesn't stop smoking?" My wife said, "Because he'd leave me if I did." I'm ashamed to admit it, but I believe she was right, such is the fear that smokers suffer when confronted with the prospect of having to stop. I now realize that many smokers don't finish the book because they feel they'll have to stop when they do. Some deliberately read only one line a day in order to postpone the 'evil' day. Now I am fully aware that many readers are only reading this book because they have had their arms twisted to do so by people that love them. Look at it this way: what have you got to lose? If you don't stop at the end of the book, you are no worse off than you are now. YOU HAVE ABSOLUTELY NOTHING TO LOSE AND SO MUCH TO GAIN!

Incidentally, if you have not smoked for a few days or weeks but aren't yet sure whether you are a smoker, an ex-smoker or a non-smoker, then don't smoke while you read. In fact, you are already a non-smoker. All we have to do is to let your brain catch up with your body. By the end of the book you'll be a happy non-smoker.

Basically, my method is the complete opposite of the so-called 'normal' method of trying to stop. The 'normal' method is to list the considerable disadvantages of smoking and say, "If only I can go long enough without a cigarette, eventually the desire to smoke will subside and I can perhaps begin to enjoy life again."

On the surface, this is a logical way to go about it, and thousands of smokers are stopping every day using variations of this method. However, the truth is that it's very difficult to succeed with this approach for the following reasons:

1. By focusing on the disadvantages of smoking we are addressing the wrong issue. We should be focused on why we smoke, not why

we shouldn't smoke. Smokers already know they shouldn't smoke, and if this knowledge were going to make them stop, it would have done so long ago. The challenge is to understand the illusory reasons we do smoke, and deal with them.
2. Some of the things we use to motivate us to abstain do make us want to quit, but they also make us want to smoke. This sounds illogical but it isn't. Take the biggest reason that smokers want to stop: health. If you see an anti-smoking commercial highlighting the dangers of smoking, it provokes an emotional response based around the fear and anxiety that it might happen to you. This in turn creates stress and the smoker's first response to stress is to want to light a cigarette. This is why so many quit smoking campaigns make it harder, not easier, for smokers to stop.
3. It perpetuates the myth that the smoker is sacrificing something or depriving himself of something when he stops. This sense of deprivation makes us feel miserable and vulnerable, which in turn makes the cigarette appear desirable. We have to use willpower not to give in to this desire and we enter that familiar cycle of wanting to smoke but not being allowed to. This deepens the misery and stress, which of course heightens the desire to smoke, and so it continues until we can eventually take no more, admit defeat and light up. The problem here is not the cigarette itself, but the desire to smoke. If the smoker retains the desire to smoke then so long as he is not smoking, he will be miserable. This poor soul doesn't ever become a non-smoker, but remains a smoker who is not allowed to smoke.

The Easy Way is basically this: to forget, for a time, the reasons we want to stop, to turn to face the cigarette and to ask ourselves the following questions:

1. What does the cigarette do for me?
2. Do I enjoy it?
3. Do I really need to go through life paying through the nose just to stick these things in my mouth and suffocate myself?

The beautiful truth is that it does absolutely nothing for you at all. Let me make it quite clear: I'm not saying that the disadvantages of smoking outweigh the advantages – all smokers know that throughout their smoking lives – I'm saying that there are NO advantages to smoking. The only 'benefit' smoking ever had – as a social lubricant – has long gone. In Canada today, smokers are considered (unjustly, in my view) the most anti-social of all addicts.

All smokers rationalize why they smoke but all of the reasons we use to explain our smoking are excuses or based on myths and fallacies.

The first thing we are going to do is to address and remove these myths and fallacies. In fact, you will quickly realize, there is nothing to give up. Not only is there nothing to give up, but there are marvelous, positive gains when you become a non-smoker, and vastly improved health and finances are just two of these gains. Once the illusion that life will never be quite as enjoyable without the cigarette is removed, once you realize that not only is life just as enjoyable without it, but infinitely more so, once the feeling of being deprived or of missing out are eradicated, then we can reconsider health and money – and the dozens of other reasons for stopping smoking. These realizations will become powerful additional aids to help you achieve what every smoker really wants – to enjoy the whole of your life free from the slavery of smoking.

Chapter 3

Why is it Difficult to Stop?

As I explained earlier, I got interested in this subject because of my own addiction. When I finally stopped, it was like magic. When I had tried to stop previously, there were weeks of black depression. There would be odd days when I was comparatively cheerful but the next day I would invariably sink back down into this pit of misery and depression. It was like clawing your way out of a slippery pit. You feel that you are nearing the top – you can see the sunshine – but begin to feel yourself sliding back down again. Eventually, to end the misery, you light a cigarette. It tastes awful, makes you even more depressed and you try to work out why you have to do it.

One of the questions I always ask smokers prior to a consultation is "Do you want to stop smoking?" In a way it's a stupid question. All smokers, including our friends in the pro-smoking lobbies would love to stop smoking. If you say to the hardest of hardcore smokers "If you could go back to the time before you got hooked, with the knowledge you have now, would you have started smoking?", "NO WAY!" is the reply.

Say to the most confirmed smoker – someone who doesn't think that smoking injures their health, who is not worried about the social stigma and who can afford it (there aren't many around these days) – "Do you encourage your children to smoke?", "NO WAY!" is again the reply.

All smokers intuitively feel that something evil has taken possession of them. In the early days it was a question of "I'm going to stop, but not today – maybe tomorrow." Eventually we get to the stage where we think that we either don't have the required amount of willpower or that there is something inherently so enjoyable about smoking that we feel that we can't enjoy life without cigarettes.

As I said previously, the problem is not explaining why it is easy to stop: *it's understanding why we believe it has to be so difficult*. In fact, the real challenge is to explain why anyone smokes in the first place, and why at one time over 60% of Canadian adults smoked.

The whole business of smoking is an extraordinary enigma. The only reason we begin to smoke is because of the influence of those already smoking. Yet every one of them wishes that they had never started. We can't quite believe that they are not enjoying it. We associate smoking with adulthood and growing up, which is all that teenaged kids aspire to. We work hard to learn to smoke and to get hooked. We then spend the rest of our smoking lives trying to stop and telling our own kids not to take it up in the first place.

We also spend the rest of our lives paying through the nose for what we now perceive as our own stupidity. The average pack-a-day smoker has to earn around $250,000 in their lifetime to finance his or her smoking habit. What do we do with that money? It wouldn't be so bad if we just threw that money out with the garbage, but we use it to systematically suffocate ourselves, congest our lungs with cancer-triggering tars and to poison our bodies with the hundreds of toxic chemicals contained in tobacco. Each day we increasingly starve every muscle and organ of oxygen, so that we become more and more lethargic. We sentence ourselves to a lifetime of filth, bad breath, stained teeth, filthy ashtrays, vile-smelling clothes and furniture and standing alone outside, banished to sub-zero temperatures. We spend the majority of our lives in situations where we can't smoke (work, church, hospitals, schools, restaurants etc.) feeling deprived. We spend our lives seeking out opportunities to smoke, planning our next cigarette, building our day around the next occasion where we'll be able to light up. And when we are smoking we're wishing we didn't have to. Looking at the cigarette thinking, "Why am I doing this?"

What sort of hobby or pastime or pleasure or habit is it that when you are doing it you wish you weren't, and that only seems desirable when you aren't doing it?

It's a lifetime of being treated by the bulk of our society (sometimes our children included) as some kind of leper and, worst of all, living with a profound sense of self-disgust. The smoker despises him or herself and their inability to control this one aspect of their lives. Every time the Federal or Provincial Government needs to balance their books and slaps another couple of dollars on a carton, every Weedless Wednesday, every time we glance at a pack and see the health warnings, every time we see an anti-smoking ad on TV, every time we feel short of breath or a pain in the chest, every time we're the only smoker in a room full of non-smokers. Having to go through life with these awful black shadows hanging over us, fear lurking permanently at the back of our minds, what does the smoker get from the cigarette? ABSOLUTELY NOTHING! Pleasure? Enjoyment? Relaxation? A prop? A boost? If any of these were true, smokers would be happier and more relaxed than non-smokers.

As I have said, the real challenge is not to explain why smokers perceive stopping as being difficult, but to explain why anybody does it at all.

You are probably saying, "That's all very well. I know this, but once you are hooked on cigarettes, it is very difficult to stop smoking." But why is it so difficult, and why do we have to do it? Smokers search for the answers to these questions all of their lives.

Some say it is because of the terrible physical withdrawal symptoms. In fact the actual withdrawal symptoms from nicotine are so mild (see Chapter 6) that most smokers go through the whole of their smoking lives not realizing they are drug addicts.

Some say that it's the taste and smell of cigarettes that keep us smoking. Nothing could be further from the truth. They are filthy, disgusting objects. Ask any smoker who suffers from the illusion that he enjoys the taste if, when he can't get his brand, he stops smoking. Of course not. Smokers would rather smoke old rope than not smoke at all. I enjoy the taste of lobster, but I never got to the stage where I had to have twenty lobsters with me everywhere I went. The truth is that we smoke *despite* the smell and taste of cigarettes, not because of it. In fact, part of the definition of nicotine addiction from the Canadian Medical Association is 'tolerance of the smell and taste of a cigarette.' What they are saying is that once we have taught ourselves to cope with the disgusting taste and smell of tobacco, it's a classic sign that you're hooked. Actually, recent research from teams out of McGill and Waterloo Universities argues that the building blocks of addiction are formed after just two cigarettes.

Some search for deeper psychological reasons to rationalize why they smoke. The Freudian analysis of the cigarette as a substitute for the mother's breast. This sounds good, but doesn't make much sense when you analyse it. Most kids start smoking to demonstrate that they are adults and no longer tied to the Mother's apron strings, which is the opposite of wanting a substitute for the breast. If it were true that cigarettes provided the feeling of safety and security then everyone would smoke. After all, we all have the same human needs to feel safe, secure, loved etc.

Some argue the reverse, that the cigarette is a badge of adulthood and independence. Again, the opposite is true. How do we demonstrate our independence by becoming dependent on a drug that enslaves us?

Some say, "It's something to do with my hands." So, why light it?

"It's oral gratification." So, why light it?

"It's the feeling of smoke going into my lungs." An awful feeling – replacing oxygen with poison – it is called suffocation.

Many believe that smoking relieves boredom, but if that were true, then smokers would never be bored. Are smokers saying that there is a magic ingredient in tobacco that is a medical cure for boredom? And if we smoke to relieve boredom, then why do we also smoke when we are not bored? What the smoker is really saying here is that the cigarette creates a distraction that allows us to forget we are bored for a moment or two.

But the same smoker will argue that the cigarette helps them to concentrate. There is a contradiction here. When we need to concentrate, we remove distractions we don't look for them. So is the cigarette a distraction or does it remove distractions? It can't do both. How is it possible that a drug which provides a distraction at 9am can miraculously remove distractions at 9:30am? It can't.

And there is another contradiction too. Smokers claim that the cigarette relaxes them and helps them to handle stressful situations. But they also claim that it helps them get going in the morning, and that it gives them a boost. How can a drug that relaxes you or relieves stress also stimulate you? This contradiction illustrates the truth about smoking. The cigarette just doesn't do any of the things we tell ourselves it does.

If cigarettes relaxed us and helped to relieve stress then smokers would be more relaxed and less stressed than non-smokers. If cigarettes helped us to get going and helped us concentrate, then smokers would be more energetic and would enjoy enhanced brain function. All athletes would be smokers, as would all university professors and Nobel Prize winners. It would be mandatory for people in stressful professions, like Air Traffic Controllers and Surgeons, to smoke. Hmmmm.

For thirty-three years my excuse was that it relaxed me and gave me confidence and courage. I also knew it was killing me and costing me a fortune. Why didn't I go to my doctor and ask him for an alternative to relax me and give me courage and confidence? I didn't in case he did. It wasn't my reason; it was my excuse.

Some say they do it for social reasons, because their friends do it. This might wash when we are twelve or thirteen, just starting out, but it doesn't make sense when we are fully-grown, independent adults.

Most smokers who think about it eventually come to the conclusion that it is just a habit. This is not really an explanation but, having discounted all of the rational explanations, it appears to be the only excuse that makes sense. Unfortunately, this explanation is equally illogical. We make and break habits every day of our lives, and some of them are very enjoyable. We have been brainwashed into believing that smoking is a habit and that habits are hard to break. Are habits hard to break? In the UK we drive on the left side of the road. Yet when I travel to Canada or the US, I need to drive on the right. So I break my UK driving habit and acquire a new habit of driving on the right. This change causes me no mental or physical anguish. In fact, it is quite pleasant to make a change from time to time. I don't miss driving on the left or develop a craving to drive on the left. It's a fallacy that habits are hard to break. We do it every day with no bother whatsoever.

So why do we find it difficult to break a 'habit' that tastes awful, that kills us, costs us a fortune, that is filthy and disgusting and that we would love to break anyway, when all we need to do is to stop doing it? The answer is that smoking is not a habit: IT IS NICOTINE ADDICTION! That is why is appears to be so difficult to 'give up'. Perhaps you feel that this explains why it *is* difficult to 'give up' – it certainly explains why smokers *believe* that it has to be difficult. This misconception arises because smokers don't understand drug addiction. It persists because smokers have been brainwashed into believing that they get some genuine pleasure or crutch from smoking and believe that they are making a genuine sacrifice when they quit.

The beautiful truth is that once you understand nicotine addiction and the real reasons you smoke, it is easy to stop smoking. Three weeks from now the only mystery will be why you found it necessary to smoke for as long as you have, and why you can't persuade other smokers of HOW NICE IT IS TO BE A NON-SMOKER!

Chapter 4

The Sinister Trap

Smoking is the most subtle, sinister trap that man and nature have ever combined to devise. What gets us into it in the first place? The thousands of adults who are already doing it. They even warn us that it's a filthy, disgusting habit that costs a fortune and kills you, but still we cannot believe that they are not enjoying it. One of the saddest aspects of smoking is how hard we have to work in order to become hooked.

It is the only trap in nature that has no lure, no bait. The thing that springs the trap is not that cigarettes taste so marvelous; it's that they taste so awful. If that first cigarette tasted wonderful, alarm bells would ring and, as intelligent human beings, we could then understand why so many get hooked and spend the rest of their lives smoking. But because the first cigarette tastes so awful, our young minds are reassured that we could never get hooked on something so disgusting, and we think that we could stop anytime we wanted to. By that stage, we're already hooked. Groundbreaking research out of McGill University has indicated that after just two cigarettes, teenagers are already developing the building blocks of nicotine addiction.

Nicotine is the only drug in nature that has the opposite effect to that which is desired. Boys usually start because they want to appear tough or cool – like Mel Gibson in Lethal Weapon or Bruce Willis in Die Hard. In reality, tough is the last thing you feel when smoking your first cigarette. You dare not inhale, and if you do, you feel dizzy and nauseous – usually within seconds. All you want is to get away from the other boys and throw the filthy things away. We don't even need the health warnings. Our bodies tell us in no uncertain terms – GET THIS POISON OUT OF ME!

With women, the aim is to be the sophisticated modern young lady. We have all seen them taking little drags on a butt, looking utterly ridiculous. Trying to copy Julia Roberts, Sharon Stone or Sarah Jessica Parker, or in years gone by, Bette Davis or Marlene Dietrich – the epitome of a successful, attractive woman.

By the time the boys have learned to look cool and the girls to look sophisticated, they wish that they had never started in the first place. Actually, I'm now of the view that no woman looks sophisticated when smoking. Notice how pictures of these beautiful, glamorous smokers never show them actually smoking, but just holding the lit cigarette? It seems to me that there is no intermediate stage between the obvious beginner and the wrinkled, pinched look of a hardcore smoker.

We then spend the rest of our lives trying to justify to ourselves why we do it, telling our children not to get caught in the trap and, at odd times, trying to escape ourselves.

The trap is so designed that we try to stop only when we have stress in our lives, whether it be health, shortage of money or just plain being made to feel like a leper and a criminal.

Because we associate stress relief with cigarettes, these stressful situations that motivate us to quit, also make us want to smoke. As soon as we stop, we have more stress in our lives. We want a cigarette but can't have one. Previously, we relied on the cigarette to relieve stress, but now we must do without.

After a few days of torture we decide that we have picked the wrong time to quit. We must wait for a period when we have less stress, but as soon as we have less stress, our reasons for quitting also diminish. Of course, that stress-free time never comes. As we leave the protection of our parents, the natural process is to set up home, find a partner, build a family and a career and so on. We perceive these things to be stressful but they are really just part of growing up and becoming adults. We tend to confuse responsibility with stress. The truth is that the most stressful period of our lives is childhood and early adolescence. This is the period of our lives when everything is new and unknown and when our world is going through profound and constant change. Yet during this time of tremendous change and stress, we are perfectly able to handle it without cigarettes or any other false props or drugs.

Smoker's lives are significantly more stressful than non-smoker's. This is because tobacco doesn't relax you or relieve stress, as the brainwashing would have you believe. Just the opposite: smoking causes smokers to become more nervous and stressed and far less relaxed than non-smokers. You don't need a degree in Biochemistry to know this, just look around – it's plain to see.

The whole business of smoking is like wandering into a giant maze. As we enter the maze our minds become misted up and clouded, and we spend the rest of our lives trying to find our way back out. I spent thirty –three years trying to escape from that maze. Like all smokers, I couldn't understand it. However, due to a combination of unusual circumstances, none of which reflect any credit on me, I wanted to know why previously it had been so desperately difficult to stop and yet, when I did finally quit, it was not only easy but enjoyable.

Since stopping smoking my hobby and, later, my life's work has been to try to resolve the many conundrums associated with smoking. It is a complex and fascinating puzzle and, like Rubik's Cube, practically impossible to solve without assistance. However, like all complicated puzzles, if you have an instruction manual and know the solution, it's easy. This book is your instruction manual to find it easy to escape from the smoking trap. I will lead you out of the maze and ensure that you never wander into it again. All you have to do is *follow the instructions*. This means what it says. If you don't follow an instruction, in effect you take a wrong turn in trying to escape from the maze. One wrong turn renders the rest of the instructions meaningless.

Let me be very clear about this: any smoker can find it easy to stop smoking, but first we need to establish the facts. No, I don't mean statistics about lung cancer, heart disease and the many other conditions caused by smoking. You are already aware of this information and if it was going to stop you from smoking, it would have done so years ago. I mean, why do we find it difficult to stop? In order to answer this question we first need to know why we smoke.

Chapter 5

Why We Smoke

We all start smoking for stupid reasons, usually because of peer pressure, but once we become aware that we're hooked why do we carry on smoking?

No smoker understands why he or she smokes. If they did, they would stop immediately and effortlessly. I have asked this question of thousands of smokers during my consultations. The correct answer is the same for all smokers, but the variety of replies is infinite. I find this part of the consultation the most amusing and at the same time the saddest.

All smokers know in their heart of hearts that they are mugs. They know that they had no need to smoke before they became hooked. Most of them can remember that their first cigarette tasted awful and that they had to work hard to learn to tolerate the disgusting smell and taste. The most annoying part is that they sense that non-smokers are not missing out on anything and that they are laughing at them (it's difficult not to on Budget Day).

However, smokers are intelligent, rational human beings. They know that they are taking enormous risks with their health and their family's future and that they spend a fortune on cigarettes during their smoking lives. Therefore it is necessary for them to develop a rational explanation to justify their smoking.

The actual reason why smokers continue to smoke is a subtle combination of the factors that I will elaborate on in the next two chapters. They are:

1. NICOTINE ADDICTION
2. BRAINWASHING

Chapter 6

Nicotine Addiction

Nicotine, a colourless, oily compound, is the drug contained in tobacco that addicts the smoker. It is the most addictive drug known to mankind, and it can take just two cigarettes to get hooked. One cigarette is enough for former smokers to get hooked again.

Every drag of a cigarette delivers via the lungs to the brain a small dose of nicotine that acts more rapidly than the dose of heroin the junky injects into his vein. (In fact, this comparison is one that the tobacco companies themselves use. In an internal memorandum dated 1971, a Philip Morris (the world's biggest tobacco company) executive wrote: *"The cigarette should be conceived not as a product but as a package. The product is nicotine.... Think of the cigarette pack as a storage container for a day's supply of nicotine.... Think of a cigarette as a dispenser for a dose unit of nicotine. Think of a puff of smoke as the vehicle of nicotine....)"*

Nicotine is a very fast-acting drug, which means that it also leaves the bloodstream quickly. Within twenty minutes of extinguishing a cigarette, nicotine levels have fallen to around half, and after an hour, to around a quarter. There is enough nicotine in each cigarette to make the average smoker want a cigarette about every forty-five minutes. This explains why most smokers smoke around twenty cigarettes a day.

As soon as the smoker puts out a cigarette, the nicotine starts to leave the body and the smoker goes into withdrawal.

At this point I must dispel a common illusion that smokers have about withdrawal. Most believe that withdrawal pangs are the terrible trauma that is experienced when a smoker isn't able to smoke, or is attempting to quit. This is not true. These pangs are, in fact, mainly mental and are caused by the illusion that the smoker is depriving himself of his pleasure or crutch.

The actual pangs of withdrawal from nicotine are so slight that most smokers have lived and died without even realizing that they are drug addicts. Fortunately it is an easy drug to kick, once you understand the nature of the addiction and accept that we are, in fact, addicted.

There is no physical pain in the withdrawal from nicotine. It is merely an empty, restless feeling, the feeling that something isn't quite right or that something is missing, which is why many smokers think it is something to do with their hands. If it is prolonged the smoker becomes anxious, insecure, agitated and irritable. It's like hunger – for a poison, NICOTINE.

Within seven seconds of lighting a cigarette the drug reaches the brain and the 'craving' ends, resulting in the feeling of relaxation and security smokers feel that cigarettes give them.

In the early days, this whole process of withdrawal and relief when replenishment occurs is so slight that we are not even aware they are taking place. When we begin to smoke regularly we think it is either because we have come to enjoy them or that we have got into the 'habit'. The truth is that we're already hooked. We don't realize it but the little nicotine monster is already inside us and its appetite is slowly but surely growing.

All smokers start smoking for a variety of mainly stupid reasons but the only reason that anybody continues to smoke, whether they be a 'casual' or a heavy smoker, is to feed that little monster.

The whole business of smoking is a series of puzzles. All smokers instinctively know that they have fallen into a trap. However, the saddest thing about smoking is that the only enjoyment a smoker gets from a cigarette is relief from the discomfort of withdrawing from the previous cigarette. All the smoker is looking for is to remove the aggravation caused by withdrawal and to attain the peace and tranquility they had before they started smoking in the first place.

You know that feeling when a neighbour's burglar alarm has been ringing all day, or there has been some other persistent, nagging aggravation? The noise suddenly stops and we experience a wonderful feeling of peace and tranquility. Actually, this peace is something of an illusion. All that has really happened is that the aggravation has disappeared and we've returned to normal. What we are enjoying is not the feeling of normality, but the ending of the aggravation.

Before we start smoking our bodies and our lives are complete. We then force nicotine into our body by smoking our first cigarette. The nicotine from that cigarette leaves the body and is replaced by that barely noticeable feeling of emptiness, a bit like hunger. This is nicotine withdrawal. If we smoke again, the nicotine is replaced and the slight emptiness disappears, and is replaced by a feeling of relaxation, satisfaction and confidence (i.e. a feeling of normality). But the nicotine from the second cigarette also leaves the body, so the slightly empty feeling returns. So we need to light another cigarette to remove that feeling and to once again feel normal. And so the smoker's cycle of withdrawal and replenishment begins. It's a lifelong chain of attempts to relieve the slight aggravation caused by withdrawal and to once again feel normal.

The whole business of smoking is like forcing yourself to wear tight shoes just to get the pleasure of taking them off.

This process is very visible and obvious to non-smokers. It's clear to them that their smoking friends and colleagues aren't happier or less stressed or more relaxed than non-smokers when they smoke. Rather, it's that smokers are less happy, more stressed and less relaxed when they can't smoke.

Because non-smokers see smoking this way, they correctly perceive no advantages to smoking. As a consequence, they have no desire to smoke. With no desire to do something, it takes no willpower not to do it.

There are three main reasons why smokers find it difficult to perceive cigarettes the way non-smokers perceive them:

1. From birth, we have been exposed to massive brainwashing telling us that smokers receive immense pleasure from smoking, or that it provides a crutch or a support to help us cope with stress. We just can't believe that smokers would spend huge sums of money and take horrendous risks with their health to do something that doesn't give them anything.
2. Because physical withdrawal from nicotine is so mild, just a slightly empty feeling in the pit of your stomach a bit like hunger, we don't think of cigarettes the same way we think about other drugs. Because it's barely even noticeable, we perceive the state of withdrawal as normal, inseparable in our minds from normal hunger or stress.
3. However, the main reason that smokers fail to see smoking in its true light is because it works back-to-front. It's when you are not smoking that you suffer that empty feeling. When you light up, it disappears, giving the impression that the cigarette is useful or functional. What we forget is that withdrawing from the previous cigarette created that empty feeling in the first place! This is the illusion of pleasure we associate with smoking. We only acknowledge the boost the cigarette gives us. What we don't acknowledge is that the previous cigarette put us down there in the first place to where we needed the boost. Non-smokers don't need the boost because they didn't get the empty feeling caused by withdrawing from the previous cigarette in the first place.

It is our inability to understand this reverse process that can make it difficult to kick this or any other drug. Fortunately, once you understand the process, it's easy.

Picture the panic of a heroin addict who has no heroin. Now picture the utter joy when that addict can finally shoot up. Non-heroin addicts don't get that panic feeling when they can't shoot up. The heroin doesn't relieve the symptoms of panic; withdrawing from the previous dose caused them.

Non-smokers don't get the empty feeling of needing a cigarette or start to panic when they can't smoke. The cigarette causes those symptoms, then the next one relieves them to provide the illusion of pleasure.

Smokers talk about cigarettes relaxing them and giving satisfaction. But how can you even notice being relaxed unless one was tense in the first place? How can we suddenly feel satisfied unless we were previously dissatisfied? Why don't non-smokers suffer from this state of tension and dissatisfaction? Why is it that after a meal non-smokers are perfectly relaxed and happy, but smokers are tense and edgy – until they feed the little monster?

Forgive me if I dwell on this subject for a moment. The main reason that smokers find it difficult to quit is that they believe that they would need to give up a genuine pleasure or crutch. It is absolutely essential to understand that there is nothing to give up.

The best way to understand the subtleties of the nicotine trap is to compare it with eating. If we are in the habit of eating at certain times of the day, we don't get hungry between meals. Only if the meal is delayed are we aware of being hungry, and even then there is no physical pain, just an empty, slightly insecure feeling which we know as: "I need to eat." The process of satisfying our hunger can be very enjoyable indeed.

Smoking appears on the surface to be almost identical. The empty, insecure feeling we know as wanting or needing a cigarette is very similar to hunger for food, although one will not satisfy the other. Like hunger, there is no physical pain and the sensation is at such a low level, we aren't even aware of it for much of the day. It's only when we want to smoke but aren't able to that we become aware of any discomfort. When we light up, the discomfort ends and we once again feel normal.

It is this similarity to eating which fools smokers into believing they get a genuine pleasure or crutch when they smoke. Sadly, the truth is that all they have done is to remove the slight feeling of discomfort caused by withdrawing from the previous cigarette. Some smokers find it difficult to accept that there is no genuine pleasure or crutch. Some argue: "How can you say there is no crutch? You've just told me that when I light up I remove the feeling of discomfort."

Although eating and smoking appear to be similar, in fact they are exact opposites:

1. You eat to survive and to be healthy, whereas smoking is the biggest cause of preventable death and disease in the history of Western civilization.

2. Food genuinely tastes good and eating can be genuinely pleasurable, where as smoking involves ingesting poisonous fumes.
3. Eating doesn't cause hunger it relieves it. Withdrawing from the nicotine contained in the first cigarette you ever smoked created a hunger for your second cigarette, and so on. Cigarettes don't satisfy the hunger to smoke, they create it and perpetuate it.

This is an opportune moment to dispel another common illusion about smoking – that smoking is a habit. Is eating a habit? If you think so, try breaking it completely. No, to describe eating as a habit is the same as calling breathing a habit. Both are essential for survival. It is true that different people satisfy their hunger at different times and with different foods, but eating itself is not a habit. Neither is smoking. The only reason a smoker lights a cigarette is to try to end the slightly empty, insecure feeling created by withdrawing from the nicotine contained in the previous cigarette. It is true that different smokers are in the habit of trying to relieve their withdrawal pangs at different times and with different brands, but smoking itself is not a habit.

Society frequently refers to the smoking 'habit' and in this book, for convenience, I also refer to the 'habit'. However, be constantly aware that smoking is not a habit; IT IS DRUG ADDICTION.

When we start to smoke we have to force ourselves to learn to cope with the poisons and the disgusting smell and taste. Before we know it, we are not only buying them regularly but we *have* to have them. If we don't, panic sets in, and as we go through life we tend to smoke more and more.

This is because, as with any other drug, the body tends to create immunity to the effects of nicotine and we therefore need to smoke more to obtain the same effect. After quite a short period, the cigarette fails to completely relieve the withdrawal pangs it creates, so that when you light a cigarette you do feel better but are still more stressed and less relaxed than a non-smoker would be – even when you're smoking.

This situation is exacerbated because, once the cigarette is extinguished, the nicotine rapidly leaves the body creating more withdrawal symptoms. This is why in stressful situations smokers tend to chain smoke.

As I said, the 'habit' doesn't exist. The real reason why every smoker keeps smoking is to feed the little nicotine monster he has created. The monster tends to need feeding in certain situations and we come to associate these occasions (or a combination of them) with smoking. The 'Big Four' smoking occasions are:

BOREDOM & CONCENTRATION – two complete opposites!
STRESS & RELAXATION – two complete opposites!

What magic drug can suddenly have the opposite effect that it had twenty minutes ago? How can a drug that relieved boredom by providing a distraction suddenly help you concentrate when you need to remove distractions?

The truth is that smoking doesn't do any of these things we tell ourselves it does. If it did, smokers would be less bored / better able to concentrate / less stressed / more relaxed than non-smokers. Even smokers will readily admit that this is not the case.

Apart from being a drug, nicotine is also a powerful poison and tiny amounts are used in many commercial insecticides. A tiny amount is all that is needed to kill. If the nicotine from one cigarette were injected directly into the bloodstream, it would kill a human in less than ninety seconds. In fact, tobacco contains hundreds of poisons, including carbon monoxide, formaldehyde, cyanide and ammonia. This shouldn't come as a surprise as the tobacco plant is from the same family as 'deadly nightshade'. A list of the ingredients contained in tobacco smoke from the BC Ministry of Health website runs to 3,000 items and 14 pages.

In case you have visions of switching to a pipe or cigars, I should make it quite clear that the content of this book applies to all tobacco and any substance that contains nicotine, including nicotine gum, patches, sprays and inhalators.

The human body is the most sophisticated machine on the planet. No species on earth, from the lowest amoeba upwards can survive without knowing the difference between food and poison.

Through a process of natural selection over hundreds of thousands of years, our minds and bodies have developed techniques for distinguishing between food and poison and have developed fail-safe methods for ejecting the latter.

All human beings are averse to the smell and taste of tobacco until they become hooked. We don't even need the health warnings to know that tobacco is poisonous. We need only to listen to our bodies. If you blow tobacco smoke into the face of any child or animal they will instinctively cough or splutter in an attempt to expel the poison.

When we smoked our first cigarette, inhaling invariably started off a coughing fit. If we managed to smoke the whole thing, we most likely experienced dizziness or nausea. These symptoms were our body's way of telling us: "YOU ARE FEEDING ME POISON. STOP IT!" This is the key moment that often decides whether we become smokers or not. It is a fallacy that weak or weak-willed people become smokers. Smokers need to be strong and strong-willed to endure the process of learning to smoke. The lucky ones are those who find the first cigarette so repulsive that they can't even go through this process. Their bodies physically can't cope with the poisons and they are cured for life.

To me this is the most tragic part of the whole business. How hard we worked to get hooked in the first place! Ironically, this is why it can be difficult to get teenagers to quit. They still find cigarettes and smoking distasteful and refuse to believe that they could ever get hooked on something so disgusting. They believe that they could stop whenever they wish. Sadly by this stage, they are already addicted. Why do they not learn from us? Then again, why did we not learn from our parents?

Many smokers believe they enjoy the taste and smell of tobacco. This, like so much else with respect to smoking, is an illusion. What we are actually doing when we learn to smoke is teaching our bodies to become desensitized to the disgusting smell and taste of a cigarette, in order to get our fix. In fact, the Canadian Medical Association defines a symptom of nicotine addiction as 'tolerance of the taste and smell.' What they are saying is that by the time you have learned to tolerate the disgusting smell and taste, it's a classic sign that you're hooked.

Ask a smoker who believes that he smokes because he enjoys the smell and taste of tobacco, "If you can't get your brand, do you abstain?" No way. A smoker will smoke anything rather than abstain. Smokers prefer their own brands because they have taught themselves to tolerate the smell and taste, but if their brand isn't available a smoker will smoke any brand in order to get his fix. This is why smokers who at first find roll-ups, cigars, menthols or pipes disgusting, over time can learn to 'like', or more accurately, tolerate them.

Smokers will even keep smoking through colds, 'flu', sore throats, bronchitis and emphysema. Enjoyment has nothing to do with it. If it did, no one would smoke more than one cigarette. There are even thousands of ex-smokers hooked on that filthy nicotine gum that doctors prescribe, and many of them are also still smoking.

During my consultations some smokers find it alarming to realize that they are drug addicts and think that this will make it harder for them to stop. In fact, it is very good news indeed, for two important reasons:

1. The reason that most of us carry on smoking is because, although we know that the disadvantages of smoking outweigh the advantages, we believe that there is something intrinsically enjoyable that the cigarette gives us. We feel that after we stop smoking there will be a void and that life will never quite be the same again. This is an illusion. The fact is that the cigarette gives you nothing apart from very slight withdrawal that you alleviate by lighting another

cigarette. By alleviating the symptoms of withdrawal, you feel like a non-smoker. In short, smokers smoke so they can feel like non-smokers. I will explain this in more detail in a later chapter.

2. Although it is the most addictive drug known to man because of the speed with which it hooks you, ironically you are never badly hooked on the drug itself. Because it is so fast acting, it also leaves the body quickly. Just twenty minutes after extinguishing a cigarette, nicotine levels drop to half. By one hour, three-quarters has gone. After just three days you are in practical terms, nicotine free. After three weeks you could do a carbon monoxide exhalation test and it would not register one single nicotine molecule.

You will ask, quite rightly, that if this is the case, then why do so many smokers find it hard to quit, and suffer through months of torture? Why do so many go through life craving cigarettes, even years after they have stopped?

The answer is the second component to the smoking conundrum – the brainwashing. The chemical addiction is easy to cope with. In fact, smokers cope with it their whole smoking lives and they cope with it so easily that they aren't even aware that they are going through withdrawal.

Most smokers go all night without a cigarette. The withdrawal pangs don't even wake them up.

Many smokers will actually leave the bedroom before they light that first cigarette; many will even eat breakfast first; increasingly people don't smoke in their homes so won't have that first cigarette until they are in the car on their way to work; some won't even smoke in the car and will have their first cigarette after they arrive at work. These smokers have gone eight or maybe ten hours without a cigarette – going through withdrawal all the while, but it doesn't seem to bother them.

Nowadays many smokers will automatically refrain from smoking in the homes, or even in the company of non-smokers. Even when I was a chain smoker I was able to go for quite long periods without smoking and it didn't bother me in the slightest. In fact, there were days, particularly in my latter years as a smoker, when I used to look forward to going home in the evening so that I could stop choking myself (what a ridiculous 'habit').

If physical withdrawal were as bad as the brainwashing would have us believe, how is it that we can go for extended periods of time without even noticing it?

Smokers have the illusion that they only suffer from withdrawal when they try to quit. In fact, smokers suffer withdrawal their whole smoking lives. It's what makes them reach for their next cigarette. It's just that this withdrawal is so slight that we don't even realize we're experiencing it.

As I say, physical withdrawal from nicotine does exist – we experience it every time we put out a cigarette – but it's not the real problem. It just acts as a catalyst to confuse us over the real problem: the brainwashing.

It may be of consolation to older smokers and heavier smokers to know that it is just as easy for them to stop as it is for 'casual' smokers. In some respects, it's even easier because heavier smokers tend not to have any illusions that they enjoy smoking.

It may be of further consolation for you to know that the rumours that occasionally circulate (e.g. "Every cigarette takes five minutes off your life.") are untrue. The human body is an incredible machine and irrespective of how many years you have been smoking, the body bounces back quickly and wonderfully, provided you haven't already contracted an irreversible smoking-related condition. It truly is miraculous. The recovery starts immediately after you put out your final cigarette. Within just twenty minutes your heart rate returns to normal and after 24 hours, the likelihood of a heart attack is reduced by half.

It is never too late to stop. I have helped to cure many smokers in their fifties, sixties and seventies, and even a couple in their eighties. All reported dramatic improvements in their health, and most of them noticed the change within a couple of days. A 91-year-old once attended our clinic with her 66-year-old son. When I asked why she had decided to stop, she replied: 'To set an example for him.' She contacted me six months later saying she felt like a young girl again.

The further the drug drags you down, the greater the relief when you quit. When I finally broke free I went from a hundred cigarettes a day to ZERO and didn't experience even one pang. In fact, it was actually enjoyable, even during the withdrawal period.

Think of nicotine addiction as the little monster. It's utterly insignificant and you can squash it like a bug. The danger of the little monster is that it feeds the big monster – the BRAINWASHING.

Chapter 7

Brainwashing and the Sleeping Partner

How or why do we start smoking in the first place? To understand this fully we need to examine the power of the mind and in particular, the sub-conscious mind or, as I call it, the sleeping partner.

We all tend to think of ourselves as intelligent human beings making conscious decisions that dictate the path of our lives but the truth is that most of our behaviour and attitudes are determined by our surroundings, upbringing and by forces of which we are largely unaware.

These forces, mostly benign, work at a sub-conscious level. As children, we absorb enormous amounts of information – good, bad, useful and utterly worthless – effortlessly and without even being aware that we are learning.

Tobacco marketing executives are well aware of the importance of the sub-conscious and the power of suggestion and they have used it for years to promote the image of smoking as normal, natural and desirable. When we are growing up we are bombarded with messages that cigarettes help us relax, concentrate and handle stress. We form the belief that cigarettes are special and precious and that we are somehow incomplete without them. You think I exaggerate? Remember those old war movies? The dying soldier is always given a cigarette to ease him peacefully and nobly to his heroic death. What's the last request of the man facing death by a firing squad? That's right – a cigarette. The subtext running beneath this seemingly innocent request is an important one. What this is really saying is: 'The most precious thing on this earth, my last thought and action, will be the smoking of a cigarette'. Of course the impact of this doesn't register at a cognitive level – but it does get filed away and absorbed by our sub-conscious. When this information is reinforced thousands of times by a variety of means (movies, TV, peers, parents etc.) we accept it unquestioningly.

You think that things have changed recently? Not a chance. Whilst TV advertising has been banned for years, the appearance of smoking in movies and on TV continues unabated. Look at Bruce Willis in *Die Hard* or Mel Gibson in *Lethal Weapon*. These movies, aimed at teenage boys glamorize smoking in a way a TV ad never could. For two hours Mr. Willis and Mr. Gibson chain-smoke their way through a myriad of death defying and heroic sequences. The subtext again is very simple: Even heroes need their little friend. What better way to show your cool and rebellious nature than to smoke?

Does this happen by accident, or is it part of a concerted strategy by tobacco companies to promote smoking to teenagers as cool, rebellious and desirable? I'm not a conspiracy theorist but it's obvious to me that if you are in a business where 15,000 of your customers die every day, then you need to replace them somehow. Given that over 90% of smokers start before their eighteenth birthday, it makes sense to market to as young a demographic as possible, without being seen to be doing so.

As a demonstration of the tobacco industry's success in promoting to children, the American tobacco giant RJ Reynolds, which for years owned Canada's third largest tobacco company, ran a campaign based on a kid's cartoon character, Joe Camel. Joe Camel took RJR's market share in the under 18 market from 0.5% to 32.8% in the first three years. In research published in the Journal of the American Medical Association, over 90% of six year olds matched the Joe Camel character with a cigarette. According to the same research, for a time, Joe Camel was as well known as Mickey Mouse amongst American pre-schoolers.

TV is no better than cinema. I recently watched an episode of the otherwise wonderful *West Wing*. Martin Sheen's character, the President of the US, when faced with a difficult decision in a stressful situation, wanders to his private study and sitting alone with the enormous burdens of his office, lights a cigarette. Once again the message being promoted: Smoking relieves stress. Even the most powerful man in the world needs his little crutch.

Think about it, what better ad could you have than actors and actresses we love and admire smoking on-screen? John Travolta, Al Pacino, Robert de Niro, Brad Pitt, Julia Roberts, Nicole Kidman, Nicolas Cage, Matt Damon, Humphrey Bogart, Lauren Bacall, Marlene Dietrich, Leonardo di Caprio, Gwyneth Paltrow…the list is endless.

I don't believe that Hollywood any longer benefits financially from working with the tobacco companies to promote smoking (though this has unquestionably been the case in years gone by – for more information on this visit the excellent www.smokefreemovies.ucsf.edu) but every time an actor lights up in a movie aimed at kids, the message that smoking is normal, desirable and glamorous is reinforced. That message is filed away in the sub-conscious and the cumulative impact of it being repeated thousands upon thousands of times during a child's formative years builds a desire for kids to experiment. Unfortunately, nicotine is so addictive that experimentation all too often leads to addiction.

True, there is publicity to counter this brainwashing, but it's a case of too little, too late. Anti-smoking campaigns fail to effectively reverse the brainwashing promoting cigarettes and smoking for two key reasons. Firstly, they tend to feature older people. Youngsters just don't care that a 60 year-old woman is smoking through a tracheotomy because it is not a present danger to them. Anyway, which teenager starts smoking with the intention of smoking for the rest of their lives? Do you think alcoholics mean to become alcoholics? Teenagers believe that they could never get hooked on cigarettes and that they could quit at any time, if they wanted to. So why would an ad featuring someone with whom they cannot identify resonate with them? Secondly, the campaigns come too late, after the teenager has already become a smoker. As with every addiction or condition, prevention is better than cure.

Health Canada does spend money on prevention but the truth is that, despite the millions of dollars spent, there are more 15-19 year olds smoking today than there were when the Canadian Tobacco Usage Monitoring Survey was first published in 1985. According to the Minister of Health's 2002 Annual Report, every ten minutes two Canadian teenagers start smoking. We can hardly characterize this as a stunning success.

The trap today is the same as when Sir Walter Raleigh fell into it. All the anti-smoking campaigns do is confuse the issue. The challenge is not so much to counter the brainwashing as it is to ensure that our children aren't subjected to it in the first place.

For an example of the power of the brainwashing to which the smoker is subjected, and the fear that it creates, one need look no further than the issue closest – in more ways than one – to the smoker's heart. Although we are acutely aware of the health risks associated with smoking, and for the most part don't argue or debate those risks (can 60,000 medical studies linking smoking with lung cancer all be wrong?), smokers point to the exceptions that prove the rule. Every smoker knows an Uncle Fred who smoked two packs a day, never had a day's illness in his life and lived until ninety. We ignore the fact that for every Uncle Fred there is a Humphrey Bogart or Steve McQueen or George Harrison or Bob Marley or Lucille Ball or Bette Davis or Errol Flynn. Every 11 minutes a Canadian dies of smoking-related causes.

I highlight this capacity for self-delusion not to try to make you feel bad – I was the worst of the lot when I was a smoker – but to illustrate the extent to which we are brainwashed into searching for any scrap of information that allows us to continue to justify our smoking.

We're even brainwashed into minimizing the problems that smoking creates in favour of demonizing other social issues that don't even begin to have as serious ramifications. As a society we get uptight about glue sniffing, heroin addiction and smoking pot. In 2003 these three activities accounted for fewer than 300 deaths in Canada. Tragic as they indisputably are, they don't come close to matching the 45,000 deaths caused by smoking.

Marijuana is often labeled as a 'gateway' drug, but in my consultations I have met literally thousands of people who have smoked pot and not one became addicted. On the other hand, over 80% of alcoholics are smokers and I have yet to meet a heroin addict who isn't a smoker. If there is a gateway drug it is nicotine.

Governments around the world have a love / hate relationship with tobacco. On the one hand, governments salivate over tobacco revenues (an estimated $8bn a year in Canada) but they know that this will be far outstripped by the future medical and other costs associated with smoking. So far, greed is winning the battle at the expense of smokers and their families.

One of the key challenges in becoming a happy non-smoker is to see through all this brainwashing and to recognize cigarettes for what they really are. Very early on in our smoking lives we unwittingly elevate the cigarette's importance and place it on a pedestal. There it remains for the rest of our smoking lives, unchallenged and omnipotent. We need to begin to ask some searching questions:

Why do I smoke?

What does the cigarette do for me?

Do I really need to smoke?

NO, OF COURSE YOU DON'T

I find this brainwashing aspect the most difficult of all to explain. Why is it that an otherwise rational, intelligent human being becomes a complete imbecile about his own addiction? It pains me to confess that out of the thousands of people I have assisted in stopping smoking, I was the biggest idiot of all.

My father was a heavy smoker. He was a strong man, cut down in his prime due to smoking. I can remember watching him as a boy; he would be coughing and spluttering in the mornings. I could see he wasn't enjoying it and it was obvious to me that something evil had possessed him. I can remember saying to my mother, "Don't ever let me become a smoker."

At the age of fifteen I was a physical fitness fanatic. Sport was my life and I was full of courage and confidence. If anybody had said to me that I would end up smoking a hundred cigarettes a day, I would have gambled my lifetime's earnings that it would not happen, and I would have gleefully given any odds that had been asked.

At the age of forty I was a physical and mental wreck from smoking. I had reached the stage where I couldn't complete even the most mundane of tasks without first lighting up. With most smokers the triggers are the normal mild stresses of life, like answering the phone or socializing. I couldn't even change the channel on the TV or a light bulb without lighting up.

I knew it was killing me. There was no way I could kid myself otherwise. But why I couldn't see what it was doing to me mentally I cannot understand. It was almost jumping up and biting me on the nose. The ridiculous thing is that I never even suffered the illusion that I enjoyed smoking. I smoked because I thought it helped me concentrate and handle stress. Now I am a non-smoker, the most difficult part is trying to believe that those days actually happened. It's like waking up from a nightmare, and that's about the size of it. Nicotine is a drug, and your senses are drugged – your taste buds, your sense of smell. The worst thing about smoking isn't the damage to your health or your finances, it is the warping of your mind. You search for any excuse to keep smoking, despite being acutely aware of how it is affecting your life.

I remember at one stage switching to a pipe, after another failed attempt to kick cigarettes, in the belief that it was less harmful and would cut down my intake.

Some of those pipe tobaccos are absolutely foul. The smell can be pleasant as most pipe tobaccos are infused with artificial aromas, but to begin with they are awful to smoke. I can remember that for about three months the tip of my tongue was as sore as a boil. A liquid gunge gathers in the bowl of the pipe. Occasionally you unwittingly bring the bowl up beyond the horizontal and before you realize it, you've swallowed a mouthful of the filthy stuff. The result is usually to throw up immediately, no matter what company you are in.

It took me three months to learn how to cope with a pipe, but what I can't understand is why, during that time, it didn't occur to me to ask myself why I was subjecting myself to this torture.

Of course, once they learn to master it, few seem as contented as a pipe smoker. Most are convinced that they smoke because they enjoy the pipe. But surely the question is why did they have to work so hard to learn to 'enjoy' it when they were perfectly happy without it?

The answer is that once we're hooked, we have to find a way to service our addiction. You need to get this very clear in your mind. You didn't get addicted to nicotine because you fell into the habit of smoking. It's the other way around. You had to get into the habit of smoking to service your addiction.

Even the expression 'giving up' is part of the brainwashing. This phrase implies tremendous sacrifice. The beautiful truth is that there is absolutely nothing to give up. On the contrary, you will be freeing yourself from this terrible slavery and achieving marvelous positive gains. We are going to start to remove the brainwashing now. From this point on, no longer will we refer to 'giving up', but to stopping, quitting or the most accurate descriptor of all: ESCAPING!

What tempted us to smoke in the first place was the influence of people already smoking; whether they're the cool kids at school, movie stars or our own family. We assume that smokers are gaining some tremendous pleasure and we fear that we are missing out on it. We work so hard to get hooked yet no smoker ever finds out what they've been missing. Every time we see another smoker, we are reassured that there must be something to smoking, otherwise all these other people wouldn't be doing it. Because he's brainwashed into believing he has made a genuine sacrifice when he quits, the cigarette continues to dominate even the ex-smoker, and makes him feel deprived. This is why people quitting using willpower are so miserable.

As a child I remember listening to the extremely popular Paul Temple detective show on BBC Radio. One of the programmes dealt with marijuana addiction. Some evil men were 'spiking' cigarettes with pot. There were no harmful effects. People merely became addicted and had to go on buying the cigarettes. I was about seven at the time and it was the first time I had heard of addiction. The very concept of it terrified me and even to this day, even though I know at a cognitive level that marijuana is not addictive I would not dare take one drag of a joint. How ironic that I should end up addicted to the worlds number one addictive drug. If only Paul Temple had warned me about that tobacco in the cigarette instead of the marijuana! Ironic too that at this time (the immediate pre-war period) tobacco companies were already aware of the addictiveness of nicotine and were experimenting with ways to increase nicotine yields. It is incredible to me that we continue to allow tobacco companies to spend millions of dollars to persuade our children to smoke, and that the government profits to the tune of billions of dollars every year.

We are about to remove the brainwashing. It is not the non-smoker who is being deprived but the smoker, who gives up a lifetime of:

HEALTH
ENERGY
WEALTH
PEACE OF MIND
CONFIDENCE
COURAGE
SELF-RESPECT
SELF-ESTEEM
HAPPINESS
FREEDOM

And what does he gain from making these enormous sacrifices?

ABSOLUTELY NOTHING! The only thing the cigarette does is remove the aggravation caused by withdrawing from the previous cigarette, so that the smoker, for a moment, feels like a non-smoker. By lighting up, he temporarily relieves the very slight feeling of emptiness and enjoys the state of relaxation and peace that non-smokers enjoy all their lives. But immediately after putting the cigarette out, the nicotine beings to leave the bloodstream and the slightly empty feeling returns. So the smoker has to light up again, and again and again.

Chapter 8

Relieving Withdrawal Pangs

As I explained earlier, smokers think they smoke to get a boost or because they enjoy it. In fact, this is an illusion. The real reason that any smoker lights up is to relieve the withdrawal pangs. The pangs are so mild that most smokers are completely unaware that they even exist.

In the very early days, we use the cigarette as a social prop. We can take it or leave it. But as the days and weeks go by, the sub-conscious begins to realize that the cigarette relieves the very slight pangs caused by withdrawing from the nicotine contained in the previous cigarette. We light up, the pangs temporarily disappear and we return to normal, like a non-smoker. This is what provides the illusion of pleasure. Of course, the non-smoker doesn't need this artificial boost because they were not suffering from withdrawal in the first place.

Because stress or mild anxiety can feel like the empty, insecure feeling caused by nicotine withdrawal, our sub-conscious starts to think that the cigarette will relieve these symptoms too. So we form the sense that the cigarette helps us relax or handle stress. There is a grain of truth to this in that we do feel better after we light up, but all we have done is to relieve the stress and discomfort caused by withdrawing from the previous cigarette. At no time has the cigarette helped us to address the real stress or source of anxiety. It has merely removed the stress caused by the previous cigarette, giving the illusion of pleasure.

As with any drug, our bodies begin to develop immunity to its effects. The more we become hooked, the more we need to smoke, and the further the cigarette drags you down. Of course the further we are dragged down, the more we need the artificial boost the cigarette provides. It doesn't take long for us to now consider the state of withdrawal as our natural state, so we need to smoke regularly to feel even a semblance of normality and we become stressed and agitated if we are unable to relieve the withdrawal by smoking. This whole process is so subtle and gradual that most smokers are completely unaware that they are hooked. Instead smokers tell themselves that they enjoy smoking or that they could quit anytime they wanted to.

As already stated, smokers tend to relieve their withdrawal pangs at times of stress, boredom, concentration, relaxation or a combination of these. This is explained in greater detail in the next few chapters.

Chapter 9

Stress

I am referring not only to the great tragedies of life but also to the minor stresses, the socializing, the telephone call, the anxieties of the homemaker with noisy young children and so on.

Let me use the homemaker as an example. This is a very rewarding, but a very stressful and sadly, thankless life. Homemakers need to juggle more tasks than even the busiest of businessmen. They need to be part driver, part cleaner, part cook, part dishwasher, part teacher, part psychologist, part soccer coach...the list is endless. How women achieve so much in a day only to wake up the following day and do it all again is beyond me. When the smoking homemaker is confronted with an additional stressful situation (for example, the car won't start), their instinct is to want to light a cigarette. She doesn't know why this is, just that it is.

What is actually happening is this. Without being conscious of it, she is already suffering mild aggravation from withdrawing from her previous cigarette. When the additional stress comes, because her sub-conscious mind associates the relief of stress with cigarettes, she wants to smoke. When she lights up she relieves the stress caused by nicotine withdrawal, and feels better. This boost is not an illusion – she does feel better – but the cigarette has only removed the stress caused by withdrawing from the nicotine in the previous cigarette. Of course, smoking a cigarette has not fixed the car so the real stress still exists. However the smoker now feels better able to cope with the stress because they are temporarily no longer going through the additional stress of withdrawing from nicotine.

This is the illusion of the cigarette as a stress reliever. It temporarily partially relieves the stress caused by the previous cigarette. But all the smoker is really doing is guaranteeing that he or she will experience withdrawal pangs again and again...

Actually, I believe that even when they are smoking and supposedly relieving stress, smokers are more stressed than non-smokers. There are so few opportunities to smoke nowadays that even when we're smoking we're stressed by the thought of not being able to do so again whenever we wish. Some smokers spend their whole day planning and creating opportunities to smoke. Talk about stress!

I promised you no shock treatment. In the example I am about to give, I am not trying to shock you, I am merely emphasizing that cigarettes create stress rather than relieve it.

Try to imagine getting to the stage where your doctor tells you that unless you stop smoking he is going to have to remove your legs. Just pause for a moment and reflect on that. Try to even begin to visualize life without your legs. Try to imagine the frame of mind of a man who, issued with that warning, actually continues to smoke and then has his legs removed.

I used to hear stories like that and dismiss them as cranky. In fact, I used to wish that a doctor would tell me that; then I would have stopped. Yet I was fully expecting any day to have a brain hemorrhage and lose not just my legs but also my life. I didn't think of myself as a crank, just a heavy smoker.

Such stories aren't cranky. That is what this awful drug does to you. As you go through life it systematically robs you of your courage and your nerve. The more it ruins your courage, the more you come to rely on the drug to restore it. We all know the panic that smokers experience when they are out late at night and running low on cigarettes. Non-smokers don't experience this fear; the cigarette creates it.

Cigarettes not only destroy your nerves, but also have many toxins that attack the central nervous system and other key organs and systems, progressively destroying your physical health. By the time the smoker reaches the stage at which it is killing him, he depends totally on the cigarette believing that it is his courage, and he cannot face life without it.

Get it clear in your mind. Cigarettes don't relieve stress; they create it. Cigarettes don't help you to calm down and relax; they cause you to be panicky and agitated. One of the most wonderful things about breaking free from this awful drug is the return of your courage, confidence and self-esteem.

Chapter 10

Boredom

If you are already smoking at this moment, you will probably have already forgotten about it until I reminded you.

Another fallacy about smoking is that it relieves boredom. Boredom is a frame of mind, not a medical condition. Are we really saying that there is a biologically active ingredient in tobacco smoke that cures boredom? If a non-smoker drank a glass of water when they were bored, would they begin to think that there was something in water that relieved boredom? Of course not.

Anyway, it's not as if the dull, gray fog of boredom is replaced by the brilliant, shining, multi-coloured thrill of excitement when a smoker lights up. Initially, you were bored. Now you are bored and smoking.

Just because smokers smoke when they're bored it doesn't mean that smoking relieves boredom. The fact is that if smoking relieved boredom, smokers would never be bored. At the very least they would be significantly less bored than non-smokers, something that is obviously untrue.

What we are saying is that the cigarette provides a momentary distraction if we are bored. If you have something to occupy your mind that isn't stressful, you can go long periods without smoking and not be at all bothered. However, if there is nothing to occupy you and you are bored, you look for something to relieve it. This is why smokers tend to smoke more when they are bored. But think about it: if a cigarette relieved boredom, then why would we need to smoke more than one?

As with so much about smoking, the truth is the opposite of the brainwashing we have been subjected to. I believe that smokers have more boredom in their lives than non-smokers because cigarettes rob them of energy and they are more lethargic. Instead of getting up and doing something when they are bored, as a non-smoker does, the smoker tends to want to lounge around, bored, relieving their withdrawal pangs.

Don't take my word for it. See for yourself. Observe smokers who are smoking because they are bored. They still look bored. The cigarette cannot and does not relieve boredom; otherwise smokers would never be bored.

Anyway, if smokers smoked to relieve boredom, then why do they also smoke when they are not bored?

As an ex-chain-smoker I can assure you that there are no more boring activities in life than lighting up one filthy cigarette after another, day in day out, year in year out.

Chapter 11

Concentration

Cigarettes do not assist concentration. That is yet another illusion.

When you need to concentrate, you automatically try to remove distractions like feeling too hot or too cold. But the smoker has another distraction: the little nicotine monster hasn't been fed and until he is, the smoker will find it difficult to concentrate for any sustained period of time. So the smoker lights up, removes the distraction caused by withdrawal from the previous cigarette, feels like a non-smoker and can concentrate.

Looking at it this way it is obvious that cigarettes don't help concentration; rather that experiencing withdrawal makes it harder to do so. Of course non-smokers aren't distracted by withdrawal pangs and therefore don't need to smoke to remove them.

There is no question in my mind that cigarettes seriously impair our ability to concentrate. Apart from the constant distraction of going through nicotine withdrawal, the progressive blocking of arteries and veins with the poisons contained in tobacco starves the brain of oxygen.

It was the concentration aspect of smoking that prevented me from succeeding when using the willpower method. I could put up with the irritability and bad temper, but when I really needed to concentrate on something difficult, I had to have that cigarette. I can well remember the panic I felt when I discovered that I was not allowed to smoke during my accountancy exams. I was already a chain-smoker and convinced that there was no way I could concentrate for three hours without a cigarette. But I passed the exams and can't even remember thinking about smoking at the time, so when it came to the crunch, it obviously didn't bother me.

If we look at the world around us, it's blatantly obvious that cigarettes don't enhance concentration or get our creative juices flowing. If they did then every Nobel prize winner on the planet would be a smoker, and research institutions would encourage their staff to smoke. Plato, Homer, Leonardo da Vinci, Michaelangelo and Galileo all seemed to operate at a rarified intellectual level without the aid of tobacco.

The loss of concentration that smokers suffer when they try to stop smoking is not due to physical withdrawal from nicotine. When you are a smoker and you have a mental block, what do you do? That's right, you light a cigarette. That doesn't cure the block so what do you do? You do what non-smokers do – you get on with it. Only this time you do so without the distraction of going through nicotine withdrawal. You work through the block – as the non-smoker does – but give the credit to the cigarette. Instead you should be blaming the cigarette for providing the distraction that caused the loss of concentration in the first place.

This is a common theme with respect to smoking. The cigarette gets the credit for everything and the blame for nothing. The moment you stop smoking, everything that goes wrong in life is blamed on the fact you've stopped smoking. The ex-smoker using willpower still believes that the cigarette aids concentration and when he has a mental block, thinks: 'If only I could light a cigarette it would solve my problem.' He then questions his decision to quit and this doubt eats away at his resolve – the first step on the way to relapse.

As a footnote to this issue, smokers who say that the cigarette helps them to concentrate are often the ones who claim that it also relieves boredom. This is interesting because when we're bored we look for distractions and when we want to concentrate we look to remove distractions. So which one is it? Does the cigarette provide a distraction or remove distractions? It obviously can't do both because they are exact opposites, yet because as smokers we unquestioningly accept the brainwashing, we tell ourselves that it can.

When I extinguished my final cigarette I went overnight from one hundred a day to zero without any loss of concentration.

Chapter 12

Relaxation

Most smokers think that a cigarette helps them relax. The truth is that nicotine is a stimulant (a very poor and inefficient stimulant, but a stimulant nonetheless). How can we say that a stimulant relaxes us?

One of the favourite cigarettes for most smokers is the one after a meal. This is because a meal is a part of the day when we can sit down, relax and relieve our hunger and thirst. At such times the non-smoker is on a real high, just enjoying the opportunity to relax and socialize. However, the poor smoker can't relax, as he has another hunger that needs to be satisfied. He thinks of the cigarette as the icing on the cake, but in reality it is the little monster that needs to be fed, and until he has been fed, the smoker can't relax.

The most uptight people on the planet aren't non-smokers but fifty year-old business executives who chain-smoke, are permanently coughing and spluttering, have high blood pressure and are constantly irritable. At this point cigarettes cease to relieve even partially the symptoms that they have created.

I can remember when I was a young accountant, bringing up a family. One of my children would do something wrong and I would lose my temper to a degree that was out of all proportion to what he had done. I really believed that I had an evil, uncontrollable demon somewhere in my character. I now know that this was true, but it was the nicotine monster rearing its ugly head, not some flaw in my make-up. During those times I thought I had all the problems of the world on my shoulders, and I wondered what I had done to deserve this miserable life of stress and misery. Now I can clearly see what the problem was. I was in control of all aspects of my life, bar one. The cigarette controlled me completely, and it was this that was the source of so much unhappiness. The sad thing is that even today I can't convince my children that it was the smoking that caused me to be so irritable. Because of the brainwashing, they still believe that cigarettes calm and relax smokers, where the truth is that they cause tremendous stress and they prevent you from relaxing.

Some years ago the adoption authorities threatened to prevent smokers from adopting children. A man rang a talk show I was listening to on the topic. He said, "This is completely wrong. I can remember when I was a child if I had a contentious matter to raise with my mother I would wait until she lit a cigarette because she was more relaxed then." A smoker views this as proof that cigarettes aid relaxation but the truth is that it demonstrates that smokers are tense when they are not smoking.

Withdrawal creates slight feelings of tension and anxiety. When the smoker lights up he removes these feelings and can relax, like a non-smoker. But as soon as we put the cigarette out, withdrawal begins and the slight feeling of tension and anxiety returns. So we need to light up again and again...

This is the saddest thing about smoking. We smoke so that we can remove the feelings of withdrawal and feel like a non-smoker.

Smoking is full of inconsistencies and inaccuracies and one of the biggest is the myth that cigarettes relax us. If they did, smokers would be more relaxed than non-smokers. This is clearly not true. In fact, even most smokers will admit that the opposite is true.

The next time you are in a supermarket and see a young mother screaming at a child, just watch her leave. Nine times out of ten the first thing she does is light a cigarette. Start watching smokers in situations where they can't smoke. You'll find that they have their hands near their mouths, or they are twiddling their thumbs, or fiddling with their hair, or clenching their jaw and grinding their teeth. Smokers aren't relaxed. They've forgotten what it feels like to be completely relaxed. This is one of the great pleasures you have to look forward to – to once again know what it feels like to be totally relaxed.

The whole business of smoking is like a fly being caught in a pitcher plant. To begin with, the fly is eating the nectar, but as the fly eats more it cannot escape. It is trapped and the plant begins to eat the fly.

Isn't it time you escaped from the nicotine trap?

Chapter 13

Combination Cigarettes

No, a combination cigarette is not when you are smoking two or more at the same time. When that happens, you begin to wonder why you were smoking the first one. I once burned the back of my hand trying to put a cigarette in my mouth when I already had a lit one there. Actually, it's not as stupid as it sounds. As I've already said, eventually the cigarette ceases to relieve the withdrawal pangs and even when you are smoking you sense that something is missing. This is the curse of the chain-smoker – whenever you need a boost, you find that you are already smoking. This is why heavy smokers often turn to drink or other drugs. But I digress.

A combination cigarette is one occasioned by two or more of our usual reasons for smoking, e.g. social functions, parties, weddings, meals in restaurants. These are examples of occasions that are both stressful and relaxing. This might appear to be something of a contradiction, but it isn't. Any form of socializing can be stressful, even with friends, and at the same time you are enjoying yourself and relaxing.

There are even situations where all four reasons are present at the same time. Driving can be one of these. If you are leaving a tense situation, like a visit to the dentist or doctor, you can now relax. But driving can also be stressful. You also have to concentrate, after all your life is on the line every time you get into your car. And if you are stuck in a traffic jam, it can be boring.

Another classic example is a game of cards. If it's a game like bridge or poker, you have to concentrate. If you are losing, it can be frustrating, which creates stress. If you go through a few hands of not pulling any decent cards, it can be boring. And while all this is going on, you are at leisure; you are supposed to be relaxing with friends. During a game of cards, all smokers will be chain-smoking – irrespective of how slight the withdrawal pangs are. Even otherwise casual smokers will smoke much more than usual. The ashtrays will fill and overflow in no time. There's a constant bluish fog hovering above the table and even the smokers will complain about how smokey the room is getting. If you were to tap any of the smokers on the shoulder and ask if they were enjoying it, they would look at you as if you were mad. It is often after nights like this, when we wake up with a mouth like a cesspit that we decide to try to stop smoking.

These combination cigarettes are often 'special' ones, the ones that we think we will miss the most when we stop smoking. We think that life will never be quite as enjoyable again. It doesn't seem to occur to us that we don't enjoy them in the first place.

Most of these so-called 'special' cigarettes come either at a time that's enjoyable anyway, regardless of whether you are a smoker or a non-smoker (after a meal, a coffee break, having a drink with friends etc.) in which case the cigarette is getting the credit for something that is fun anyway, or after a period of abstinence (after a meal, a coffee break, the first of the day, after a long flight etc.) where we are enjoying not the cigarette, but the ending of the irritation of needing to smoke. This is explained in more detail in the next chapter.

Chapter 14

What am I 'Giving Up'?

ABSOLUTELY NOTHING! The thing that makes it difficult to quit is the fear that we are sacrificing something or depriving ourselves of something. The fear that life will never be the same without our 'little friend'. The fear that we won't be able to relax, or handle stress or concentrate.

The effect of the brainwashing is to delude us into believing that we are weak and fragile and that we need something to help us through the stresses and strains of life. We think that when we stop smoking, we stop living. We believe that stopping smoking will leave a void in our lives.

Get it clear in your mind: CIGARETTES DO NOT FILL A VOID – THEY CREATE ONE.

These bodies of ours are the most sophisticated machines on the planet. Whether you believe in a divine creator, a process of evolution and natural selection or a combination of both, it is safe to assume that whatever created us is many times more intelligent than we are. If we were meant to smoke, we would have been designed with a filter to screen out the thousands of toxins contained within tobacco smoke.

In fact, our bodies are provided with foolproof systems to enable us to distinguish between food and poison. We don't even need the health warnings on cigarette packs; our bodies know instinctively that we are being poisoned. When we smoke our bodies send us warning signals in the form of the cough, dizziness and nausea. We ignore these warning signs at our peril.

The beautiful truth is that there is nothing to 'give up'. Once you get rid of the little monster in your body, and the big monster in your mind you will neither want nor need cigarettes.

Cigarettes do not improve meals. They ruin them. They destroy your sense of smell and taste. As a smoker, all you can think about is why everyone else is eating so slowly and when it will end, so that you can smoke. Like I said, it's not so much that we enjoy smoking, it's that we get miserable and anxious when we can't. It doesn't seem to occur to us that non-smokers don't experience this misery and stress.

Because many of us start smoking on social occasions when we are young and a little shy, we begin to believe that we can't enjoy social occasions without a cigarette. This is nonsense. Cigarettes systematically attack your nervous system, robbing you of confidence. The best example of the fear that cigarettes instill in smokers is their effect on women. Many women are fastidious about their appearance. They wouldn't dream of going out to a big social event not looking their best, and smelling beautiful. Yet knowing that their breath smells like a stale ashtray appears not to deter them in the least. I know it *bothers* them greatly – many hate the smell of their own hair and clothes – yet it doesn't *deter* them. Such is the fear that this awful drug instills in people.

Cigarettes do not help social occasions; they destroy them. Excusing ourselves every half-an-hour to go and stand outside alone in the freezing cold, smoking half a cigarette, wondering what on earth we are doing and why, stubbing it out in frustration, trying to hide the evidence with a quick spray of breath freshener, going back inside – only to go through the exact same ritual half-an-hour later. Being constantly self-conscious wondering whether other guests can smell the smoke on you and see the nicotine stains on your teeth and fingers.

Not only is there nothing to give up, there are wonderful positive gains to be had from breaking free from the slavery of smoking. When smokers think about quitting they tend to concentrate on health, money and the social stigma associated with smoking in twenty-first century Canada. These are obviously valid and important issues, but I personally believe that the greatest gains from escaping are psychological, and they include:

1. The return of your confidence and courage
2. Freedom from the slavery of drug addiction
3. Not to have to go through the rest of your life being despised by society and, more importantly, despising yourself

Not only is life better as a non-smoker, it is infinitely more enjoyable. I do not only mean you will be healthier and wealthier. I mean you will be happier and enjoy life far more.

The incredible gains you achieve when you become a non-smoker are discussed in the next few chapters.

Some smokers find it difficult to understand the concept of the 'void' I mention, and the following analogy might assist you.

Imagine having a painful cold sore on your face. I've got this marvelous ointment. I say to you, "Try this stuff." You rub the ointment on, and the sore disappears immediately. A week later it reappears. You ask, "Do you have any more of that ointment?" I say, "Keep the tube. You might need it again." You apply the ointment and hey presto, the sore disappears again. Every time the sore reappears, it gets larger and more painful and the period of remission gets shorter and shorter. Eventually the sore covers your whole face and is excruciatingly painful. It is now returning every half hour. You know that the ointment will remove it temporarily, but you are very worried. Will the sore spread over your whole body? Will the periods of remission disappear altogether? You go to your doctor. He can't cure it. He just wants to prescribe you more ointment.

By now you depend completely on the ointment. You never go out without checking that you have a tube and if you are going abroad, you make sure that you have several tubes with you. Now, in addition to the worries about your health, I'm charging you $100 per tube. You have no choice but to pay.

Then you read in a newspaper that this isn't just happening to you; many other people are suffering from the identical problem. A researcher has discovered that the ointment doesn't actually cure the sore it merely pushes it beneath the surface of your skin. Far from curing it, it is the ointment that has caused the sore to grow. All you have to do to get rid of the sore is to stop using the ointment. The sore will soon disappear on its' own.

Would you continue to use the ointment?

Would it take willpower not to use the ointment? If you didn't believe the article you had read in the newspaper, there might be a few days of apprehension, but once you realized that the sore was getting better, the need or desire to use the ointment would go.

Would you be miserable? Of course you wouldn't. You had an awful problem, which you thought was insoluble. Now you have found the solution. Even if it took a while for the sore to disappear entirely, each day as it improved, you'd think "Isn't it marvelous? I'm not going to die this terrible death."

This was the magic that happened to me when I put out my final cigarette. Let me make one point quite clear in the analogy of the sore and the ointment. The sore isn't lung cancer, or arteriosclerosis, or emphysema, or bronchitis, or angina, or asthma or coronary heart disease. These are also caused by the ointment, but in addition to the sore. It isn't the hundreds of thousands of dollars that we burn, or the lifetime of bad breath and stained teeth, the lethargy, the wheezing and coughing, the countless times we are punished because we are not allowed to smoke and the countless times we are punished when we are. It isn't the lifetime of being despised by a society that seemed happy for you to get hooked in the first place, or the lifetime of despising yourself. These are all in addition to the sore. The sore is the fear created by that barely noticeable slightly empty, insecure feeling that says, "I want a cigarette." Non-smokers don't suffer from this fear and one of the sweetest things about breaking free from the slavery of smoking is to no longer have your life dominated by fear.

It was as if a great mist had suddenly lifted from my mind. I could see so clearly that the panic feeling of wanting a cigarette wasn't some kind of weakness in me, or some magical quality in the cigarette. Withdrawing from the first cigarette caused that panic feeling; and each subsequent one, far from relieving the feeling, perpetuated it. At the same time I could see that all these other 'happy' smokers were going through the same nightmare that I was.

For the first time in my smoking life, my fear of quitting was replaced by a feeling of excitement about how wonderful it would be to break free!

Chapter 15

Self-imposed slavery

Usually when smokers try to stop they quote health, money and the social stigma associated with smoking these days as the prime motivators. The sheer, unremitting slavery of smoking doesn't even occur to us.

We quite rightly view slavery as a great evil, yet every smoker lives the life of a slave, every day they remain a smoker. We seem oblivious to this slavery for the most part, and feel that it is somehow normal. It is far from normal. We were lucky enough to have been born free. Of all the basic human values, surely freedom is the most basic and most important? Who could conceive of anything as stupid as giving away this priceless gift in order to be enslaved to a drug that doesn't even get you high?

Increasingly, smokers are being pushed outside into the cold by society. Anti-smoking by-laws increasingly restrict where and when we can smoke. This bothers smokers, but it doesn't stop them. Ironically, these types of restrictions can make it harder, not easier, to quit. The reason for this is that because these days it is very difficult for smokers to smoke when they want, they go through periods of enforced abstinence throughout the day. As I mentioned, many 'special' cigarettes come after a period of abstinence during which the 'itch' to smoke has grown and grown. When at last the smoker can scratch the 'itch' and light up, the relief is enormous. In effect, these types of smoking restrictions make smokers believe that every cigarette is precious, and that the most important thing on the planet is the next cigarette. However, to a non-smoker it is obvious that the thing the smoker is getting from the cigarette is temporary relief of the aggravation of needing to smoke.

As an aside, it is interesting to note and also ironic that cigarettes only seem precious to us when we aren't smoking. When we are smoking, we can take it or leave it, or we are barely even aware that we are doing it. It's only when we can't do it that it seems appealing. This makes nicotine unique in the field of drug addiction. Alcoholics, heroin addicts, cocaine addicts and even pot smokers like the effects that their drug gives them and they enjoy those effects for their own sake. The tobacco smoker only ever removes the feelings of withdrawal created by the previous cigarette. What an unrewarding addiction.

This trend of increased restrictions on smoking is set to continue. Already it is virtually impossible to smoke anywhere in BC, and all of the Provinces have implemented or are in the process of implementing similar anti-smoking by-laws. Gone are the days when you could just light up in a friend's home or a restaurant. Even many smokers have a self-imposed restriction that they won't smoke in their own home. Smokers assimilate these restrictions into their routines out of necessity, but surely the question we should be asking is: 'Why?' What is it that the cigarette gives us that is so wonderful that we are prepared to give up our freedom and be treated like a second-class citizen?

I hated being dominated and controlled in this way. I was in control of every area of my life except for smoking. The cigarette was deciding where I would go, what I would do, when I would do it and with whom I would do it.

I remember during my smoking days, every time I went to church, it was an ordeal. Even during my own daughter's wedding, when I should have been standing there a proud father, what was I doing? I was thinking, "Get on with it and get it over so that I can go outside and smoke."

I can also remember playing indoor bowls – our equivalent of curling, I suppose – in the winter and pretending to have a weak bladder so that I could nip off for a quick smoke. No, this wasn't a fourteen year-old schoolboy but a forty-year-old Chartered Accountant who was supposed to be having fun. How pathetic. Even when I was playing, I wasn't enjoying it. Even before we started a match I was looking forward to the end so that I could smoke again, yet this was supposed to be my way of relaxing and enjoying myself.

I can't even begin to remember how many meals smoking ruined for me. It's funny that we tell ourselves that we enjoy the one after a meal, but the truth is that smoking ruins meals because all you can think about is wolfing down your food as quickly as possible so that you can get back to smoking.

To me, one of the tremendous joys of being a non-smoker is to be free from that slavery, to be able to enjoy the whole of my life, not spending half of it not smoking and wishing I could and the other half smoking, wishing I didn't have to. This is a tremendous burden that the smoker carries around with them and it feels wonderful when at last it is lifted from your shoulders.

Chapter 16

I'll save $x a week...

I cannot repeat often enough that it is the brainwashing that makes it difficult to quit. Many smokers don't realize this so they need to use variations of the willpower method. The more brainwashing we can remove before you start on your wonderful new life free from the slavery of smoking, the easier and more enjoyable you will find the process.

One of the biggest areas of brainwashing is money. Occasionally I meet someone whom I think of as a confirmed or hardcore smoker. By my definition, a confirmed smoker is somebody who can afford it, doesn't believe it injures his health and isn't worried about the social stigma. (There aren't many around these days.)

I do not look for confrontations with smokers – I was one and remember all too well how defensive I would get when the subject of smoking was raised – but they often approach me. If it's a young man, I say to him, "I can't believe you are not worried about the money."

Usually his eyes light up. If I had attacked him on health grounds or the social stigma, he would have felt at a disadvantage, but on money – "Oh, I can afford it. It's only $x a week and I think it's worth it. It's my only vice or pleasure," etc.

If he's a pack a day smoker, I say to him, "I still cannot believe you aren't worried about the money. You will need to earn around $300,000 in your lifetime to finance your addiction. What are you doing with that money? You are not even setting light to it or throwing it away. You are actually using that money to ruin your physical health, to destroy your courage and confidence and to suffer a lifetime of slavery. These are all priceless and irreplaceable, so long as you remain a smoker. It's like paying an assassin to kill you. Surely that must worry you?"

It becomes apparent at this point, particularly with younger smokers, that it is the first time they have ever considered smoking as a lifetime expense. For most smokers the cost of a pack is bad enough. Occasionally we work out what we spend in a week, and it's alarming. Very occasionally (and only when we're thinking about stopping) we calculate what we spend in a year and it's frightening, but over a lifetime – it's unthinkable.

The confirmed smoker with whom I'm having the discussion almost always counters with the 'encyclopedia salesman' trick. "It's only $x a week, and I can afford it." I know this trick well, having used it myself for years.

I then say, "I will make you an offer you cannot refuse. You pay me the cost of a year's smoking now, and I'll provide you with free cigarettes for the rest of your life."

If I were offering to take over his $300,000 mortgage for $3,500, he would have my signature on a contract like a shot. I have been making this offer on TV and Radio and in my books for nearly twenty years, and yet not one confirmed smoker (please bear in mind that I am not talking to someone such as yourself who plans to stop, but someone who has no intention of stopping) has taken me up on it. Why not? Is it because, like every other smoker on the planet, confirmed smokers would really rather be non-smokers?

Often at this point in my consultations, a smoker will say, "Look, I am not really worried about the money aspect." If you are thinking along these lines, ask yourself why you aren't worried. In other areas of our lives we go to great trouble to save a couple of dollars. We fill up with gas on specific days when we know the price is lower. We clip coupons. We wait until our favorite stores go on sale. We make sure we claim every last cent on our taxes. Yet here we are spending tens, if not hundreds of thousands of dollars for the privilege of poisoning ourselves to death.

The answer to this puzzle is this. Every other decision that you make in your life will be the result of an analytical process. We gather information, analyze it, weigh up the pros and cons of the various courses of action available and make a rational, fact-based decision. From time to time we get it wrong, but at least the process is a rational one. Whenever any smoker weighs up the pros and cons of smoking, the answer is the same: STOP SMOKING YOU FOOL! We can do this exercise a thousand times and a thousand times the answer would be the same.

We have two options at this stage: to sacrifice the cigarette, or sacrifice rationality. So we sacrifice rationality. We sense that we are not smoking because we want to or because we like it, but because we think we can't stop. We have to keep our head in the sand and believe the brainwashing, because otherwise we feel stupid being a smoker.

Try to take your head out of the sand for a moment. Smoking is a chain reaction. Withdrawing from your first cigarette made you smoke the second. Withdrawing from the second made you smoke the third and so on. Actually, the first cigarette you ever smoked cost you everything you have ever spent on cigarettes. That was one very expensive cigarette! Equally, your next cigarette will cost you everything you will ever spend in the future on cigarettes. If you do not break the chain, you will be a smoker for the rest of your life. Now estimate how much you would spend on smoking for the rest of your life. The amount will vary from individual to individual, but for the purposes of this exercise let us assume it is $50,000.

You will shortly be making the decision to smoke your final cigarette (not yet please – remember the initial instructions). All you have to do to remain a happy non-smoker is not to fall for the trap again. That is, do not smoke that first cigarette. If you do, it will cost you $50,000.

If you think that this is a trick way of looking at it, don't kid yourself. Just work out how much money you would have saved if you hadn't smoked your first cigarette.

Actually, this is the only sensible and accurate way to look at the financial cost of smoking.

Just think how wonderful you would feel if you won $50,000 on the Lotto. You would be dancing with joy! So start dancing because with the decision you have made to escape from the smoking trap, you have just saved yourself $50,000.

This is a great deal of money, and you should quite rightly celebrate this windfall, but the truth is that a substantially improved financial status is the smallest and least important of the gains you earn when you break free from smoking. You are also giving yourself the gifts of life and freedom. These are truly priceless, and they just aren't available to smokers.

During the three-day period of withdrawal you may be tempted to have 'one more' final cigarette. Of course that 'one more' will lead to another and another and soon enough, you'll be back smoking as you are now. It will help if you remind yourself that the first cigarette will cost you $50,000 (or whatever your estimate was). Would you spend $50,000 to get re-addicted to a drug that doesn't even get you high?

If you are ever in the company of 'happy' smokers who tell you how much they enjoy it, just tell them you know an idiot called Allen Carr who, if you pay him a year's smoking money in advance, will provide them with free cigarettes for life. Perhaps you can find me someone who will take up the offer.

Chapter 17

Health

This is the area where the brainwashing is at its peak. Smokers think they know the risks of smoking. They don't.

Even in my case, when I was expecting my head to explode at any moment and honestly believed I was prepared to accept the consequences, I was still kidding myself.

If in those days I had taken a cigarette out of the pack and an alarm started to sound, followed by a voice saying, "OK Allen, this is the one! Fortunately you get a warning and this is it. If you smoke another cigarette your head will explode," do you think I would have lit that cigarette?

There is absolutely no doubt in my mind that I would *not* have lit that cigarette. In addition, I would have been immensely relieved to have received the warning and happy that my head was not going to explode.

I did what every smoker on the planet does throughout their smoking lives: I closed my mind, prayed it wouldn't be me, kept my head firmly in the sand and hoped that I would wake up one morning with no desire to smoke. Smokers can't allow themselves to think about the health risks because if they do, even the illusion of enjoyment disappears.

This explains why the shock tactics used by Health Canada and the anti-smoking lobby are so ineffective. It is only non-smokers who can bring themselves to watch these horrific ads. It also explains why smokers, recalling Uncle Fred who smoked forty a day until he was ninety, will ignore the millions of smokers who are cut down in their prime every year because of this poisonous weed.

About six times a week I have the following conversation with smokers (usually younger ones):

ME: Why do you want to stop?
SMOKER: I can't afford it.
ME: Aren't you worried about the health risks?
SMOKER: No, I could step under a bus tomorrow.
ME: Would you deliberately step under a bus?
SMOKER: Of course not.
ME: Do you look both ways before crossing a road?
SMOKER: Of course I do.

Exactly. The smoker goes to a lot of trouble not to step under a bus and the odds are hundreds of thousands to one against it happening. Yet the smoker risks the near certainty of being crippled by smoking and seems oblivious to the risks. Such is the power of the brainwashing.

I remember one famous British golfer who wouldn't travel to North America to play because of his fear of flying. Yet he would chain-smoke round the golf course. Isn't it strange that if we felt there was the slightest fault in an aircraft, we wouldn't go up in it, yet we accept the one-in-two odds that smoking will kill or cripple us? And what is our reward for taking this truly staggering risk? ABSOLUTELY NOTHING.

In the recent beef scare in Alberta, consumers stopped eating beef altogether because of an infinitesimal risk that they would contract the human strain of mad cow disease. Not one person became ill or died, yet look at the lengths people would go to in order to avoid begin exposed to this virtually non-existent risk. During the SARS outbreak, which killed 42 people out of a population of around 6 million, tourism was decimated and the whole of Ontario was gripped by fear. I recall seeing pictures of people going about their business wearing surgical masks. The concept of a smoker wearing a surgical mask to avoid a 1:250,000 SARS risk while simultaneously subjecting himself to a 50% chance of premature death or disability due to smoking is an interesting one. Whilst the death of 42 people is a tragedy, we would do well to remember that smoking kills that number every ninety seconds.

Smoking is easily the biggest cause of preventable death in the world. It is estimated that every year around 6 million deaths are caused by smoking. Sometimes it can be difficult to even begin to get our head around something of that scale. To give you a comparison, this is like having an incident of the scale of September 11th every four hours, twenty-four hours a day, 365 days a year.

Another common myth about smoking is the smoker's cough. Many of the younger people who come to see me are not worried about their health because they don't have a smoker's cough. The truth is that smokers who don't have a cough are the ones who should worry the most. A cough is one of nature's fail-safe methods for expelling foreign matter and poisons from the lungs. The cough itself is not a disease; it is a symptom. When smokers cough it is because their lungs are trying to get rid of the cancer-triggering tars contained in tobacco smoke. When they don't cough, the poison remains in their lungs, and this is when they can cause cancer and the many other horrendous diseases associated with smoking. Smokers tend to avoid exercise and get into the habit of shallow breathing in order not to cough. I used to believe that my smoker's cough was going to kill me. In truth, by expelling much of the filth from my lungs, it probably saved my life.

Just think of it this way. If you had a nice, new car and allowed it to rust without bothering to do anything about it, that would be pretty stupid. It wouldn't be the end of the world though. A car is only money and you could always buy another. Your body is the vehicle that carries you through life. You only get one. It's cliché that our health is our most valued asset. How true that is, as any sick millionaire will tell you. Who could conceive of a more ridiculous pastime than to spend a fortune for the privilege of poisoning the vehicle upon which your very life depends?

Wise up. You don't have to do it and remember: it is doing ABSOLUTELY NOTHING FOR YOU.

Just for a moment take your head out of the sand and ask yourself, if you knew for certain that your next cigarette would be the one that triggered off the cancer in your body, whether you would actually smoke it. Forget the disease itself (it's difficult to imagine something so painful) but imagine that you have to go to Mount Sinai or Princess Margaret or St. Paul's to suffer through the endless rounds of chemo. Now you are not planning the rest of your life. You are planning your death. What is going to happen to your family and loved ones? How would it feel to have your hopes and dreams smashed to a pulp in a second? Your whole life snatched from you to be replaced by emptiness, terror and an excruciatingly painful death? How could you even begin to explain to your children?

The saddest part of my job is that I often see people to whom this has happened. Of course, they are just like you and me, they never thought it would happen to them either, but it does. The worst thing that happens isn't even the disease itself, it's the knowledge that they only have themselves to blame and the guilt they feel towards their innocent families. All our lives as smokers we say, "I'll quit tomorrow." But tomorrow never comes, does it?

Those poor smokers all say the same thing: "If only I could turn the clock back..." Sadly, this is the one thing they can't do.

You have a golden opportunity to save your life by breaking free from this awful addiction and the limitless pain and suffering it brings to so many millions of lives. You have a choice. Make no mistake; if you choose to continue to smoke after reading this book, you'll be a smoker for the rest of your life. Is this really the future you are choosing for yourself and your family?

At the beginning of this book I promised you no scare tactics. If you've already decided to become a non-smoker, this does not fall into that category. If you are still in doubt, skip the remainder of this chapter and come back to it when you have read the rest of the book.

Volumes of statistics have already been published about the damage that cigarettes can cause to the smoker's health. The trouble is that until he decides he wants to stop, the smoker goes to great lengths to avoid being exposed to such information. Even the graphic health warnings on the pack are a waste of time because the smoker doesn't even register them. And if he does see the warning it is likely to cause anxiety and stress, which will make him want a cigarette.

Smokers tend to think of the health hazard as a hit-or-miss affair, a bit like Russian roulette. Get it into your head: the deterioration to your health is already happening. Every time you take a drag you are breathing cancer-triggering fumes deep into your lungs, and lung cancer – horrific as it is – is by no means the worst of the killer diseases that cigarettes cause or contribute to.

While I was still smoking I had never heard of arteriosclerosis or emphysema. I knew the permanent wheezing and coughing and the increasingly frequent attacks of bronchitis and asthma were a direct result of my smoking. But though they caused me real discomfort, the pain wasn't too bad.

I confess that the thought of contracting lung cancer terrified me, which is probably why I just blocked it from my mind. It's amazing how the fear of the horrendous health risks associated with smoking are overshadowed by the fear of stopping. It's not so much that the fear of quitting is greater, just that it's a more immediate one. The fear of contracting lung cancer is a fear of something that might happen in the future, so we can distance ourselves from the risk and the fear it creates. Who knows? I might not get it. Surely I will have quit by then?

We tend to think of smoking as a tug-of-war. On the one side we have the fear that it's killing us, costing a fortune and making us a slave and an addict. On the other side, it's our pleasure or crutch. It never occurs to us that these perceived 'benefits' of smoking are really just more thinly-disguised fears: the fear that I won't be able to have fun, relax or handle stress. Of course both sets of fear are caused by the cigarette. Non-smokers have none of these fears.

As I have said before: it's not so much that we enjoy smoking, but that we get miserable when we can't.

Think of a heroin addict deprived of his drug and going through withdrawal. He is miserable, stressed, panicky and experiencing severe physical symptoms. Now picture that addict's utter relief when he shoots up and is able to remove those awful symptoms. Non-heroin addicts don't suffer that panic feeling. The heroin causes it. The subsequent dose partially relieves the symptoms, but also ensures that addict will go through withdrawal again. So the addict shoots up again to remove the symptoms and the cycle of addiction continues. Why is all this so obvious with other people's addictions, but not our own?

Non-smokers don't get anxious, panicky or stressed when they can't smoke. The cigarette causes those symptoms and the next cigarette partially relieves them. But the smoker withdraws from that cigarette too, and the need to smoke returns. So the smoker has to light up again and again.

The fear of contracting lung cancer scared me but didn't make me quit because I thought it was like walking through a minefield. You either got away with it or you didn't. It didn't even occur to me that I didn't have to walk through the minefield in the first place. I felt that I knew the risks and that it was my own business and nobody else's. If a non-smoker ever tried to make me aware of those risks I would defend my rights vigorously, using the evasive tactics all addicts adopt to attempt to justify the unjustifiable.

'You have to die of something.'
Of course you do, but is that a logical reason for deliberately shortening your life? If you could choose what to die of believe me, it wouldn't be a smoking-related disease.

'Quality of life is more important than longevity.'
Exactly. Are you suggesting that the quality of life of an alcoholic or heroin addict is better than that of someone who is not addicted to alcohol or heroin? Do you really believe that a smoker's quality of life is better than a non-smoker's? The smoker loses on both counts – his life is shorter and far more miserable.

'My lungs probably suffer more damage from car exhaust fumes than from smoking.'
Not even close to being true, but even if it were, would you go out of your way to deliberately ingest as many exhaust fumes as possible? And would you pay for the privilege?

THAT'S WHAT SMOKERS EFFECTIVELY DO!

Think of that next time you see a smoker inhale good and deep on one of those 'precious' cigarettes!

I can understand why the congestion and the risks of contracting lung cancer didn't help me to quit. I could cope with the former and close my mind to the latter. As you are already aware, my method is not to scare you into quitting, but the complete opposite – to help you to realize that there is nothing to give up and that your life will be many times more enjoyable free from the slavery of smoking.

However, I do believe that if I could have seen what was happening inside my body, this would have helped me quit. Now I'm not referring to the shock technique of showing the smoker's lung next to that of a non-smoker (I figured that both subjects were pretty dead). Anyway, it was obvious to me from my nicotine stained teeth and fingers that my lungs were unlikely to be a pretty sight. Provided they kept functioning, they were less of an embarrassment than my teeth, breath and fingers – at least no-one could see or smell my lungs.

What I am referring to is the progressive clogging up of our arteries and veins and the gradual deterioration of every muscle and organ caused by depriving them of oxygen and other nutrients. Even worse is that we replace these nutrients with poison and deadly compounds such as carbon monoxide.

Like the majority of motorists, I don't like the thought of dirty oil or a dirty oil filter in my car's engine. Can you imagine buying a brand new Cadillac and never changing the oil or filter? Or even worse deliberately adding impurities that you know will ruin the engine? That is precisely what we do to our bodies when we become smokers.

Until very recently, the tobacco industry denied that nicotine is addictive (to this day the word 'addictive' does not appear on US health warnings) or that smoking caused lung cancer, heart disease, emphysema etc. The industry and its apologists hide behind an argument based on something called etiology. Their argument goes something like this: because we know that many things (possibly thousands) might contribute to the formation of cancer cells, it is impossible to blame one thing (i.e. the cigarette), so long as even one other so-called confounding factor is present. You can never be certain, they argue, which caused the cancer. Using this as a model, it is impossible to prove that banging your head against a brick wall causes headaches, so long as another co-factor (listening to Swiss yodeling music, for example) is present.

Whilst I strongly support the right of everyone to have their own opinion, to argue that smoking doesn't cause these diseases is stupid and dangerous. I also find it incredibly callous and disrespectful of the millions of smokers who have paid the ultimate price.

One needs only to see the mountain of cigarette butts outside the cancer wards of hospitals around the country to see the link between the two.

The statistical evidence in support of the dangers of smoking is so overwhelming as not to need further debate here. No one ever scientifically proved to me exactly why, when I bang my thumb with a hammer, it hurts. I soon got the message.

I must emphasize that I am not a doctor, but I didn't need to be to know that my congestion, my permanent cough, my frequent asthma and bronchitis attacks were directly related to my smoking. This was confirmed to me in the strongest possible way when I quit smoking and all of the symptoms either disappeared or improved dramatically. You don't need to be a doctor – or a rocket scientist – to know that smoking is bad for you. The only question in the smoker's mind is whether they can survive it or whether it'll kill them.

In my view, the most devastating damage the smoker experiences is to his immune system. Every species on the planet is under constant attack from germs, viruses, parasites etc. The best defence we have is our immune system, which routinely protects us from these types of attacks. But how can our immune system function effectively when we are starving our body of the oxygen and nutrients it needs to thrive and survive? How can it work properly for you when it is under constant attack from the poisons contained in tobacco smoke? It's bad enough that smoking causes so many life-threatening conditions, but what is worse is that it on top of this, it also works, like AIDS, to brutalize our immune system making us less able to fight off other diseases and conditions.

Many of the adverse effects that smoking had on my health, some of which I had been suffering from for years, did not become apparent to me until I quit.

While I was busy despising those idiots and cranks who would rather lose their legs than quit smoking it didn't even occur to me that I was already suffering from arteriosclerosis myself. I attributed my gray complexion to my natural colouring and an unhealthy aversion to exercise. I didn't realize that it was due to the blocking up of my capillaries caused by smoking (incidentally along with smelling a lot nicer, a vastly improved complexion is one of the first things that people will notice about you when you quit, and it usually happens within a week or so). I had varicose veins in my thirties, which have disappeared since I stopped. About five years before I quit I began to have this weird sensation in my legs. It wasn't a sharp pain, just a persistent, restless, slightly sore stiffness. I would get Joyce to massage my legs every night. About a year after I quit I realized that I hadn't needed the massage.

About two years before I quit I would occasionally get violent pains in my chest, which I feared must be lung cancer but now assume to have been angina. I haven't had a single attack since I quit.

When I was a child I used to bleed profusely from cuts. This frightened me. No one explained to me that bleeding was a natural and necessary part of the healing process and that the blood would clot when it needed to. Later in life I would sustain quite deep cuts yet hardly bleed at all. This brown / red gunge would ooze from the cut.

The colour worried me. I knew that blood was supposed to be bright red and I assumed I had some sort of blood disease. However I was pleased about the consistency because it meant that I no longer bled so profusely. Not until I quit did I learn that smoking thickens the consistency of your blood and that the brownish colour was due to the lack of oxygen. It didn't particularly bother me at the time because I was blissfully ignorant, but today with hindsight, it is this that scares me the most about smoking. I used to deny that smoking caused heart disease. In fact, it's a miracle our hearts can stand up to the punishment. Being required to pump this ever-thickening gunge through ever-narrowing vessels without ever once missing a single beat. It made me realize, not how fragile we are, but how robust, strong and ingenious that incredible machine is!

I had liver spots on my hands at forty. In case you don't know, liver spots are those rather unsightly brown or white spots that very old people have on their face or hands. I tried to ignore them, assuming that they were a symptom of early senility brought on by my hectic lifestyle. Five years after I quit I was conducting a clinic in Raynes Park when an attendee mentioned that when he had quit previously, his spots had disappeared. I had completely forgotten about mine and, to my astonishment, they too had disappeared.

For as long as I could remember, I would see stars if I sneezed or stood up too quickly. If I was in a bath and stood up I would get dizzy, as if I was about to black out. I never related this to smoking. In fact I was convinced that everyone felt this way and that I was normal. About ten years ago an ex-smoker told me about this and it dawned on me that I no longer experienced any of these conditions related to circulation. When I was a smoker I could never get my fingers or toes warm in winter. No matter how long I spent indoors by the fire, my extremities would remain stone cold. I quit in July 1983 and have never been cold since, as my circulation bounced back remarkably after thirty-three years of abuse.

You might conclude that I am somewhat of a hypochondriac. I think I probably was when I was a smoker. One of the great scams of smoking is that we are led to believe that the cigarette gives us courage when in fact it leaves your courage, your nerve and your self-confidence shot to pieces. I was shocked when I heard my father say that he had no wish to live to be fifty. Little did I realize that twenty years later, I'd be saying the same. I had completely lost my *joie de vivre*. You might conclude that this chapter has been one of necessary, or unnecessary, doom and gloom. I promise you that it is the exact opposite.

When I was a child I used to fear death. I used to think that smoking removed that fear (I know now that it doesn't, just that as a smoker you have to learn to ignore it). Smoking also gave me a new fear though: A FEAR OF LIVING!

Now my fear of dying has returned. It doesn't bother me. I realize that it only exists because I have rediscovered my love of life. I don't brood over my fear of dying any more than I did as a child; I'm far too busy having fun and living life to the full to dwell on it. The odds against me living until I'm a hundred are pretty slim, but I'll try, and I'll enjoy every precious moment.

There were two other advantages on the health side that never occurred to me until I had stopped smoking. One was that I used to have persistent nightmares that I was being chased. I can only assume that this was triggered by the slightly empty, insecure feeling of withdrawal and then exaggerated by my sub-conscious. Now the only nightmare I ever have is that very occasionally I dream that I am smoking. This is quite a common dream among ex-smokers. Some worry that it shows a deep seated sub-conscious desire to smoke, but I think the fact that it's a nightmare shows that you are happy not to have to smoke any more.

When I described being 'chased' every night in a dream, I mistakenly typed 'chaste'. Perhaps this was a Freudian slip but it does lead me conveniently into the second advantage. At clinics, when we are discussing the impact of smoking on concentration I often ask, "Which organ in the body has the greatest need for a good supply of blood?" The stupid grins, usually on the faces of the men in the group, would indicate that they had missed the point. However, they were absolutely right. Being a reserved Englishman, I find the subject of sex a little embarrassing, and I have no intention of doing a miniature Kinsey report by detailing the adverse effect that smoking had on my own sex life, or on those of other ex-smokers with whom I have discussed it. Again, I was not aware of the impact of smoking on sex drive and on performance. I had attributed my sexual prowess and activity, or rather lack of it, on advancing years.

However if you watch natural history programmes as I do, you will be aware that the first rule of nature is survival and the second is reproduction. Nature ensures that reproduction is not successful unless both partners are physically healthy and able to provide the appropriate food, shelter and protection for the offspring. Man's ingenuity has enabled us to bend these rules somewhat, however I know for a fact that smoking causes impotence. I can also assure you that when you are fit and healthy you'll enjoy sex much more and more often.

The purpose of this chapter has not been to scare you into wanting to quit smoking. If scare tactics were going to work, they would have done so a long time ago. What I have attempted to do is to demonstrate that the brainwashing closes our minds to the true physical cost of smoking, and that life is so much more enjoyable without carrying this tremendous burden of fear around with you.

The effect of the brainwashing is that we tend to think like the man who, having fallen off a 100-storey building, is heard to say as he passes the fiftieth floor, "So far, so good!" We think we've got away with it up until now and another cigarette won't make the difference.

Try to see it the other way. The 'habit' is a lifetime's chain of fear, filth, disease, misery and slavery, each cigarette creating the need for the next. When you start smoking, you light a fuse. The trouble is, YOU DON'T KNOW HOW LONG THE FUSE IS. Every time you light a smoke you are one step nearer to the bomb exploding. HOW WILL YOU KNOW IF IT'S THE NEXT ONE?

Chapter 18

Energy

Most smokers are aware of the effect that this process of clogging up and depriving the body of oxygen and nutrients has on their overall health. However, they are not so aware of the impact it has on their energy levels.

One of the subtleties of the smoking trap is that the effects it has on us, both mental and physical, happen so gradually that the changes are almost imperceptible to us, and we consider them to be the normal signs of getting older.

It is very similar to the impact of poor eating habits. The potbelly appears so gradually that it causes us no alarm. We look at people who are overweight and shake our heads wondering how on earth they could have allowed themselves to reach that state.

But suppose it happened overnight. You went to bed trim, not an ounce of fat and a six-pack stomach. You awoke the following morning, thirty pounds heavier, with no muscle definition and a gut that puts your plans to go to the beach on hold indefinitely. Instead of waking up feeling fully rested and full of energy, you feel miserable and lethargic. If that happened you would be panic-stricken, wondering what awful disease you had contracted overnight. Yet the disease is the same. The fact it took twenty years to get there is irrelevant.

So it is with smoking. If I had a time machine that could transport you forward in time just three weeks to experience the mental and physical benefits of quitting, that is all I'd need to do to persuade you to quit. You would think: "Will I really look and feel that good?" Actually, what it really amounts to is, "Have I really sunk this low?" I emphasize that the benefits are not only physical; you will have tons more energy, confidence, courage and self-esteem. You'll also be more able to relax, concentrate and handle stress.

As a teenager I remember rushing around just for the hell of it. I had so much energy. It was fantastic! Then for thirty-three years I was permanently tired and lethargic. I used to struggle to drag myself out of bed in the morning, and after my evening meal it was all I could do to lie on the sofa in front of the TV. I'd usually be asleep within minutes. Because my father used to be the same, I thought this behavior was normal. I thought that only young kids and teenagers had energy, and that middle age started in the early twenties.

Shortly after putting out my final cigarette, the congestion that I had felt in my lungs for years disappeared along with my smoker's cough. My attacks of bronchitis and asthma stopped overnight, never to return. However something truly even better also happened – all the more delightful because it was so unexpected. I started waking up at seven in the morning feeling completely rested and full of energy actually wanting to exercise, jog and swim. At forty-eight I couldn't run a step or swim a stroke. My sporting activities were confined to such intensely athletic pursuits as lawn bowling and golf, for which I had to use a golf cart. Today, at age sixty-eight I jog two to three miles a day, work out for thirty minutes in the gym and swim twenty lengths. It's great to have energy, and when you feel mentally and physically strong, it feels great to be alive.

Unfortunately I don't have a time machine, so I can't show you how you will look and feel in three week's time. However, you will instinctively know that what I'm saying is correct. Grasp this wonderful opportunity and enjoy the benefits of breaking free from this unremitting, unrewarding addiction. Begin to let yourself get excited about this marvelous thing you are doing for yourself. USE YOUR IMAGINATION!

Chapter 19

It Relaxes Me and Gives Me Confidence

This is the very worst fallacy of all about smoking, and for me it ranks alongside the ending of the slavery as being the greatest benefit to quitting – not to have to go through your whole life with the permanent feeling of insecurity that smokers suffer from.

Some smokers find it hard to believe that the cigarette actually causes that insecure, slightly panicky feeling you get when you are out late at night and realize you are running out of cigarettes. This is because we have been brainwashed into believing that smoking relieves this feeling. But non-smokers don't ever have that feeling, so the only conclusion we can come to is that the cigarette creates it. We fall for a con trick: we acknowledge the slight boost that the cigarette gives us by partially removing the slight feeling of emptiness and insecurity when we light up, but we conveniently forget that it was withdrawing from the previous cigarette that created those symptoms in the first place.

As a smoker the only thing we look forward to is the next opportunity to smoke, and we go out of our way to create such opportunities. This burden creates even more stress for the smoker on top of the existing stress of going through permanent nicotine withdrawal and the stress of bombarding your body with hundreds of toxic chemicals twenty times a day.

It's blatantly obvious to non-smokers that smoking is one of the more stressful and least relaxing pursuits. Even when smokers are smoking they aren't relaxed, unless they're in a situation where they can light up whenever they wish. This perhaps explains why so many smokers have problems with alcohol; they are forced to spend time in places where they are able to smoke. This attracts smokers to bars, one of the few places it is still possible (in some places) to smoke. You only need to see the smoke-filled rooms of AA meetings to appreciate the link between tobacco and alcohol. This also explains the smoker's love of bingo halls!

It is truly ironic that we look to the cigarette to relax us when in fact it creates the stress in the first place. Smoking for relaxation is like drinking a bottle of gin to get sober.

When I finally broke free from the smoking trap I was astonished to realize that I was far more relaxed and far more confident as a non-smoker. Such is the brainwashing that I thought that I would never be able to relax without a cigarette. The truth is that as a smoker, I didn't know how it felt to really relax because I was in a permanent state of stress caused by smoking. And I was certain that cigarettes gave me confidence. I now realize that this was also an illusion. Because I got panicky when I couldn't smoke, I assumed that the cigarette gave me courage and confidence. It never occurred to me that non-smokers don't have that panic feeling and they therefore don't need the artificial boost (of removing the symptoms of withdrawal created by the previous cigarette) the cigarette gives.

In the last years of my smoking, I was a bit of a nervous wreck. I refused to have a medical, because I was terrified of what it would reveal. If I wanted to buy life insurance or private health coverage I insisted on a 'no medical' product and paid far higher premiums as a result. I hated visiting hospitals, doctors and dentists. I also had a terrible fear of the future and of aging – as a smoker, I didn't feel I was entitled to a future.

I didn't relate any of this to my smoking, but when I stopped I suddenly acquired the confidence and courage to face these issues head on. Nowadays I look forward to every day. Of course, bad things happen in my life – this is the human condition – and I am subject to the normal stress and strains, but it is wonderful to have the confidence and courage to deal with them. And the improved health, energy and freedom make the good times more enjoyable too.

Chapter 20

Those Sinister Black Shadows

Another of the great joys of breaking free from the slavery of smoking is to be free from the sinister black shadows that lurk at the back of a smoker's mind.

All smokers sense they have been trapped and to make a bad situation tolerable, we have to close our minds to the ill effects of smoking. For most of our lives smoking is virtually automatic, but those black shadows are always lurking in our sub-conscious minds, never very far beneath the surface.

There are many marvelous advantages to becoming a happy non-smoker. Some of them are pretty obvious – vastly improved health, a much-improved financial status and ending to the slavery of smoking – but such was my fear of life without cigarettes that I was prepared to ignore these obvious advantages and search desperately for any flimsy excuse to keep smoking.

We can get very creative when looking for an excuse to smoke and I was at my most creative when I was actually supposed to be trying to quit. This creativity was triggered by the fear and misery I felt by having to use willpower. Smokers can't block their minds to the health and financial aspects to smoking – they are just too big and too obvious to ignore – but I still struggle to understand how I could have blocked my mind to the sheer slavery of smoking. Spending half of my life not smoking, wishing I could, and the other half smoking, wishing I didn't have to.

In the last chapter I mentioned the incredible joy I experienced when I rediscovered my energy and confidence but this pales into insignificance next to the joy I felt when at last those sinister black clouds that for years had been hanging over me, disappeared forever, leaving me for the first time in my adult life a free man.

Smokers are not the weak willed, spineless jellyfish that anti-smokers (and even some smokers themselves) believe. I knew that I was strong-willed and I was in control of every other aspect of my life. I loathed myself for being dependent on something I despised so much and that I knew was ruining my life and my family's future. I cannot even begin to describe to you the utter joy of being free from these sinister black shadows, the dependency and the self-loathing. I can't tell you how nice it is to be able to look at smokers not with a feeling of envy, but with a feeling of pity for them and a sense of elation that you have broken free and are no longer trapped.

The last two chapters have dealt with the considerable advantages of being a non-smoker. In the interests of fair play and in a desire to give a balanced account, the next chapter lists the advantages of being a smoker.

Chapter 21

The Advantages of Being a Smoker

Chapter 22

The Willpower Method of Stopping

It is an accepted 'fact' in our society that it is very difficult to stop smoking. Even books advising you how to do so usually start off by telling you how difficult and unpleasant the entire quitting process is. The truth is that if you go about it the right way, i.e. follow the instructions in this book, it is ridiculously easy. I can understand why people might question that statement but let us consider it in detail for a moment.

If your aim is to run the four-minute mile, that's a challenge. You will have to undergo years of extremely rigorous training and even then, you might be physically incapable of doing it. In fact until Roger Bannister broke the four-minute barrier, it was considered impossible.

As a smoker about to attempt to quit, you might feel that you're about to attempt the impossible, but really all you need do is not light your next cigarette. After all, no one forces you to smoke. Unlike food or drink, cigarettes are not necessary for survival. So if you want to stop, why would it be difficult? In fact, it isn't. It is smokers who make it difficult by using the Willpower method. I define the Willpower Method as any method that makes the smoker feel that he or she is making a sacrifice. Let's look at this in more detail.

You never decided that you would become a smoker for life. You experimented with a few cigarettes and because they tasted so awful, you believed that you could never get hooked and were convinced that you could stop whenever you wished.

Before we realize it, we're buying them and we begin to feel uneasy if we don't have cigarettes close at hand or if we are going into a situation where we won't be able to smoke. Smoking, very quietly but very definitely, has become part of our lives. We always have our cigarettes close to hand and we begin to believe that they help us relax, concentrate, handle stress etc. We come to rely on the cigarette to give us a 'boost' in a wide variety of situations. We conveniently ignore the many contradictions that surround smoking. Like the fact we use a cigarette as a stimulant in the morning to help us get going, and as a relaxant in the afternoon to help us 'take the edge off'. It also doesn't occur to us that non-smokers seem to get on perfectly well without them. Whether we openly admit it or not, soon we are smoking because we don't think we can stop.

Research out of the University of Waterloo and McGill have shown that addiction takes place very quickly, but because it is so subtle (unlike, say, heroin addiction where the effects of the drug are plain to see) it can take smokers years to realize that they are hooked. This is because we are brainwashed into believing that we smoke because we enjoy it. This is distorted thinking: because we get miserable when we can't smoke, we assume it gives us great pleasure when we do.

Usually it is only when we try to stop for the first time that we realize we have a problem. The first attempts to stop are more often than not in the early days and are triggered by a shortage of cash as a student or by a realization that we are short of breath playing sports.

These 'trigger' events are stressful in themselves, and ironically, it is during times of stress when our need to smoke is its greatest. We are therefore attempting what we perceive to be an extremely stressful undertaking (quitting) at a time when we are already stressed and 'needing' to smoke. We quickly conclude that doing without our 'crutch' at a time of such stress is not an option (it never occurs to us that the cigarette is causing the stress), so we begin to look for an excuse to smoke. We tell ourselves that it 'wasn't the right time' to quit. So we decide to wait until there is less stress or no stress in our lives before trying again. Of course, this gives us the perfect excuse to keep smoking indefinitely because so long as you are smoking, you will have stress. If we ever do have a period when we aren't stressed we don't quit because we need the stress to provide the motivation to do so.

This becomes a common pattern among what we call 'serial quitters'. On the one hand we sense that smoking is stressful, but during our whole lives we have been brainwashed into believing that cigarettes relieve stress. This is tremendously confusing for smokers and it is the confusion that creates the fear about quitting and that prevents us from seeing the situation as it truly is. We believe that if we have the requisite amount of Willpower we will be able to muscle through these issues, but of course Willpower is useless because it doesn't help the smoker to resolve the smoking dilemma and remove the desire to smoke. As a consequence, the Willpower quitter is not really a non-smoker but a smoker who is not currently allowed to smoke. This is why relapse is so common among people who quit using Willpower – they never remove the desire to smoke. They believe that the cigarette gave them something and that they are now depriving themselves of that something. It is this sense of deprivation and sacrifice that keep the desire to smoke alive. Think about it, who is more likely to relapse: someone that doesn't want to smoke or someone that does?

Quite simply, the key to being a happy non-smoker is to remove the desire to smoke. With no desire to smoke, it takes no Willpower not to do so. So long as Willpower quitters don't understand this, they will continue to have a desire to smoke and will need to use Willpower to combat that desire.

After a while of trying and failing to quit, most smokers begin to rely on the possibility that they will suddenly wake up one morning with no desire to smoke. We hear stories and urban myths about Fred or Jane or John or Betsy to whom this happened (e.g. 'I had a bout of the 'flu and afterwards found I didn't want to smoke any more').

Don't kid yourself. I have investigated these rumours whenever I've heard about them and they are rarely as simple as they appear. Usually the smoker has been mentally preparing himself to quit for months beforehand and uses the abstinence imposed upon him from being unwell as the trigger to launch an attempt.

More often in the case of people who stop 'just like that' they have suffered some kind of shock that has jolted them into action. Perhaps a close friend or relative has just died from a smoking-related condition or they have had a scare themselves. They tell people, "I just decided to quit and that was it' because it shows them to be decisive, action oriented, no-nonsense go-getters. Far better than admitting that you quit because you were terrified of remaining a smoker.

Please don't misunderstand me. I am not criticizing such people. Frankly, I'll support anything that helps people quit. However the problem I have with such scare tactics is that they tend not to last. As the weeks and months go by, the ex-smoker forgets how frightened they were. Because they have not removed the brainwashing or really dealt with their desire to smoke, after a period of time the cigarette begins to look attractive. Weeks or even months into their quit, they find themselves wanting to smoke and having to use Willpower not to do so. Sadly, this usually ends with relapse. The ex-smoker tells themselves that they'll 'just have one' to prove that they've kicked it or 'to see what it's like'. Of course, they get hooked even faster this time around and are left kicking themselves in anger and frustration at having fallen into the same trap again.

Let's consider in greater detail the flaws in the Willpower method and why quitting using Willpower (and I consider all other methods as Willpower) is so difficult and unpleasant.

For most of our lives we bury our head in the sand about smoking, but every so often something happens to trigger an attempt to quit. As an initial step we weigh up the pros and cons of smoking. This confirms what we have known all along: by any rational assessment there is only one conclusion, STOP SMOKING!

If you were to sit down and give points out of ten to all of the advantages to stopping and do a similar exercise with the advantages of smoking, the total point count for stopping would far outweigh the count for remaining a smoker. Even hardcore smokers tend not to dispute this.

However, although the smoker knows he would be better off as a non-smoker, he believes that becoming one will involve making a tremendous sacrifice. Although this is an illusion, it is a *powerful* one. The smoker doesn't know why, but cigarettes seem to be very precious to us, and we seem to need them, in good times and in bad.

For years he has been subjected to brainwashing that cigarettes are precious and this illusion has been reinforced by his physical addiction to nicotine, which causes him to feel uneasy when he can't smoke. On top of this he now has to deal with even more powerful brainwashing of 'how difficult it is to quit'.

Every smoker has heard horror stories of people who have quit for months but are still desperately craving a cigarette. Then there are the bitter ex-smokers who seem intent on sharing every second of their agonizing experience with you. Smokers are also aware of the stories about people who haven't smoked for years relapsing and becoming instantly re-addicted. Anti-smoking and Quit Smoking TV ads showing smokers in advanced stages of cancer and emphysema, yet who cannot quit, add to the confusion. If those poor smokers can't quit, then what chance do I have?

So instead of starting this wonderful journey with a sense of excitement and anticipation, we start with a sense of doom and gloom, misery and depression. Sometimes we even tell our family, friends and colleagues, "Look I'm going to try to quit so I'm going to be irritable and cranky for a few months. Try to bear with me."

So there we are, about to attack this major project, filled with doom and gloom, fear, misery and depression. Convinced that it's going be difficult and unpleasant and sure that we are going to fail anyway. With this frame of mind, most attempts are doomed to failure before we even start. To be honest, I find it amazing that anyone quits with this approach.

Let's assume that this poor smoker manages to survive a few days without smoking. His mind now begins to play tricks on him. There's no physical pain, but it feels like something is missing. This feeling grows and grows and begins to obsess the smoker. We're not sure what it is we need, but we do feel sure that the cigarette will provide it. We have created a psychological need to smoke, and the only way we can overcome it is to use Willpower. We try to deal with it by making an attempt not to think about smoking but, of course, this merely guarantees that you think about it more. Soon the only thing we can think about is smoking, and we begin to say things like:

1. Life's too short. Look at September 11th; we could all die tomorrow. I could get run over by a bus. I've probably left it too late anyway. They say that everything gives you cancer these days etc.
2. I've picked the wrong time. I should have waited until the holidays started. I should have waited until the holidays finished. I should have waited until New Year's Eve. I should have waited until...
3. I can't concentrate. I'm irritable. My friends and family don't like me when I'm like this. Some people are just born to be smokers...(this one kept me smoking for thirty-three years)

At this stage, the smoker usually admits defeat and caves in. When he lights up a kind of schizophrenia takes over. On the one hand there is the illusion of relief at being able to do something that he has been 'depriving himself' of. On the other hand, the cigarette tastes awful and the smoker profoundly resents having to smoke it and can't understand why he is doing it. This is why the smoker thinks that he lacks Willpower. In fact, it isn't a lack of willpower that is the problem, but a conflict of wills. It is this conflict that is at the root of the smoker's dilemma: every smoker wants to quit, but every smoker wants to keep smoking.

The smoker fails to quit not because he doesn't have enough willpower but because he has failed to resolve the conflict of wills. As a result of this failure to resolve the conflict he is forced to revert to the status quo. Given the information he has at his disposal, this is a fairly rational decision. What's the point of being healthy if you're miserable? What's the point of being rich if you're miserable? Surely it is far better to have a shorter, sweeter life than a longer, more miserable one?

Fortunately this is not true – just the reverse. Life as a non-smoker is not only longer but is infinitely more enjoyable. If this weren't true, I can assure you, I'd still be smoking (correction – I'd be dead, but you take my point).

The misery and the subsequent 'craving' experienced by smokers trying to quit using willpower is nothing to do with physical withdrawal from nicotine. True, it's withdrawal that often triggers off the misery, but the 'craving' is in the mind and is caused by doubt and uncertainty. Because the smoker has started off by feeling that he is making a sacrifice, he begins to feel deprived. It can be stressful to be deprived of something we want. Because the smoker associates smoking with stress relief, as soon as he quits, he wants to smoke. However, because he is supposed to be quitting, he can't smoke, so the feeling of deprivation and misery grows. As a smoker, he would have cheered himself up with a cigarette but of course, this is the one thing he can't do, and so it goes on until finally the poor smoker puts himself out of his misery by lighting up. This dynamic explains why many willpower attempts last literally minutes.

Another problem with the willpower method is that success is defined in negative terms. If it is your objective not to smoke for the rest of your life, then how do you know if you've succeeded until you've lived the rest of your life? This makes it hard for people using the willpower method to get closure and to move on with their lives. Instead the majority of them are plagued by doubts about whether they have succeeded and about how or when they will know that they have truly broken free. This is why so many willpower quitters feel vulnerable at social occasions or during periods of stress, sometimes even years after putting out their final cigarette.

Whilst this is truly miserable for the willpower quitter, their struggles help us to confirm that the misery or 'craving' is nothing to do with nicotine. It is not possible that these people can continue to crave nicotine years after it has left their body.

These smokers are waiting for something to happen and at the same time, hoping that it won't. This is a pretty miserable state of affairs. How much fun can it be going through life hoping nothing will happen?

As I have said, the very real misery that these willpower quitters suffer from is entirely mental, and is caused by the doubt. There is no pain, but they are still obsessed with smoking. This is heartbreaking because their lives remain dominated by the cigarette, even though they are no longer smoking. If you'll excuse the crude comparison, they are the equivalent of the AA's 'dry drunk'. It's hardly surprising that these are some of the unhappiest people you are likely to meet, or that we look at them and form a terrible fear of quitting and becoming one of them.

As the doubts fester, the fear begins to set in:

'How long will the cravings last?'
'Will I ever be happy again?'
'Will I ever want to get out of bed in the morning?'
'Will I ever enjoy a meal again?'
'How will I ever cope with stress?'
'Will I ever enjoy a social occasion again?'

The smoker is waiting for things to improve, but so long as he feels deprived and miserable, things tend to get worse, not better. And, of course, all the while the cigarette is looking more and more desirable.

The smoker then tells himself that he'll 'just have one' and that everything will then be alright; but there is no such thing as 'one' cigarette. As soon as he puts that cigarette out, the nicotine begins to leave the body and the old empty, insecure feeling (i.e. the physical symptoms of nicotine withdrawal) reappears. Almost immediately, a little voice at the back of his mind says, "Light another."

Fearing that he'll get hooked again (too late, he already is) he doesn't light up immediately, but waits for a few hours, days or even weeks, until he thinks it's 'safe'. He's on the slipperiest of slippery slopes. Most admit defeat and are soon smoking full-time again: only now they feel angry, frustrated, guilty and stupid in addition to feeling miserable.

Even smokers who succeed with the Willpower Method tend to find the process difficult, unpleasant and have to be constantly vigilant, often for years after they've quit. The reason for this is that they never truly get to grips with the brainwashing. Long after the physical aspect of the addiction has disappeared, the desire to smoke remains, prolonging – sometimes indefinitely – the 'cravings' and so the feeling of misery and deprivation lingers. Eventually, if he can survive for long enough without cigarettes, the willpower quitter begins to accept that life goes on and that life without cigarettes might even become tolerable. This is one of the great tragedies of the willpower quitter – they never get to celebrate their achievement and to enjoy their freedom from the slavery of smoking.

It's true that many people stop smoking with the Willpower Method, but I feel that this does not, on its own, define success. Success in the smoking cessation context is when you are happy to be a non-smoker, and when you are able to enjoy the health, happiness and freedom to which this most wonderful of achievements entitles you.

The truth is that with willpower, there are far more failures than successes. According to data from the Health Canada website, success rates using Willpower range from 2-5% for so-called 'Cold Turkey' (even the name is more brainwashing, likening barely noticeable nicotine withdrawal to the savage symptoms experienced by heroin addicts). Success rates for other quit methods are difficult to gauge, but are 5-8% for nicotine replacement therapy and 8-12% for Zyban or Wellbutrin. For the statisticians among you, these figures are taken from Cochrane's Review of Abstracts and are based on 12-month continuous abstinence data.

Looking at it another way, the most 'successful' variant of the Willpower Method has an 88% failure rate at twelve months, and the least successful (and ironically, the most popular) a 98% failure rate. Our clinics would close in a month if they delivered these kinds of results.

The reason for this lack of success with the Willpower Method is obvious to me. None of these interventions help smokers understand why they smoke, or deal with the psychological desire to light up. So long as the desire to smoke remains, the smoker will struggle to break free. The desire can and does remain with many willpower quitters for the rest of their lives, and this explains why they remain vulnerable even years after they've quit.

They continue to believe that they enjoy smoking, but that they have deprived themselves by quitting. As I have often said, enjoyment doesn't come into it. It never did! If enjoyment were the reason that people smoked, no one would smoke more than one. We assume that we enjoy them because we have to. We'd feel stupid if we continued to smoke and did not 'enjoy' it. That's why many of the cigarettes we smoke, we're barely even aware we're smoking. If every time we lit up we had to be acutely aware of the smell, the taste, the consequences and that this might be the one that triggers the lung cancer, then even the illusion of enjoyment would disappear.

Watch smokers when you get a chance. It's clear that they don't particularly enjoy it. You'll see that they are only happy when they are not aware they're smoking. Once they become aware, they get uncomfortable, self-conscious and apologetic.

Keep it simple. We smoke to feed that little nicotine monster. Once you have purged him from your body and the brainwashing from your mind, you'll have neither the need nor the desire to smoke.

Chapter 23

Beware of Cutting Down

Many smokers resort to cutting down either as a stepping-stone to quitting or as an attempt to control the little monster. Many people who have never smoked a cigarette in their life endorse this strategy.

As a stepping-stone to stopping, cutting down is fatal. It is our attempts to cut down that can keep us trapped for life.

Usually, cutting down follows a failed attempt to quit. After a few hours or days of abstinence using willpower, the smoker says something like, "There's no way I can quit so I'll cut down and just smoke the special ones."

Terrible things happen:

1. You keep the little monster alive wanting to be fed as before, but you are only feeding him periodically. This forces you to experience the psychological 'craving' to smoke more often and with more intensity.
2. You spend your whole life looking at your watch, waiting for your next opportunity to smoke.
3. You have the worst of all worlds. You are still a smoker, but you have to use willpower as if you were quitting!
4. When you smoke as much as you want you rarely feel that you enjoy any of them – you're smoking because it's just what you do. However, when you cut down, self-imposed abstinence creates the feeling that every cigarette is precious.

Again, all this is obvious when you think about it. When we cut down, we are abstaining from smoking whenever we want. We still have the desire to smoke say, every 45 minutes, but we are limiting ourselves to one every couple of hours. During that time our desire to smoke builds and the longer we wait to scratch the 'itch', the more 'enjoyable' it seems when we can at last scratch it. Of course, this is also an illusion because what we are 'enjoying' when we smoke after a period of abstinence is not the cigarette, but ending the state of wanting or needing it. This is evident throughout our smoking lives. So many 'special' cigarettes come after a period of abstinence – the first of the day, the one after a meal, the one after a long flight, and so on. The longer this perceived period of 'suffering' between cigarettes; the greater the illusion of relief or 'pleasure' when we can finally light up.

The main difficulty of stopping smoking is not the chemical aspect of the addiction. That's easy. Smokers go through nicotine withdrawal every night when they go to sleep and it doesn't bother them in the slightest. The 'cravings' that terrify us so profoundly are, in fact, so mild they don't even wake you up. In the morning, most smokers will actually leave the bedroom before they light up. Many will eat breakfast. Because so few people smoke in their homes these days, many will wait until they're on their way to work before lighting up.

Most smokers go between eight and ten hours every night without a cigarette and it doesn't bother them. Interestingly, many of them couldn't do this during the day. They'd be pulling their hair out. Yet the withdrawal we experience is identical, irrespective or whether we're awake or asleep.

No, our obsession with the chemical side of the addiction and the terrible physical 'cravings' are a red herring. The real problem is psychological. Ironically, all smokers and nearly all doctors know this, yet still we believe that the solution is a pill or a patch. I have yet to come across another medical field where the success rates for pharmacological treatments are so poor yet they remain the treatment of choice for so many.

The challenge that smokers face is to counter the brainwashing we have all been exposed to. A major part of the brainwashing is the idea of the cigarette as a reward or special treat or prop or crutch. Cutting down reinforces this illusion. It leaves you feeling miserable and deprived for extended periods (i.e. when you are abstaining) and this convinces you that the most precious thing on earth is the next cigarette. Even though we might smoke less for a time (in my experience, cutting down never lasted more than a day or so), but during that time you are more enslaved than ever. The cigarette dominates your whole life.

There is nothing sadder than a smoker trying to cut down. He suffers from the junky's distorted thinking that the less he smokes the less he'll want to smoke. In fact, the reverse is true. The less he smokes, the longer he endures the psychological itch to smoke and the more he treasures finally being able to scratch the itch.

A slightly odd twist to cutting down is that the smoker often becomes more aware of the taste, which he invariably finds distasteful. It doesn't stop him smoking, but he does begin to wonder why he is doing it. Like chemical addiction, taste is a red herring. We often find that our most precious cigarettes are the ones that taste the most foul. The first of the day is a classic example. For many smokers, the first of the day is the most important, yet it's the one that has them coughing and spluttering the most.

It is essential to remove all the illusions about smoking before you smoke a final cigarette. Unless you've removed the illusion that you enjoy the taste of certain cigarettes, there will be no way of proving it after you become a non-smoker without getting hooked again. So, unless you are already smoking, light one up now. Take six big drags, inhaling each drag as deeply into your lungs as you can. Now ask yourself what it is about the taste that you enjoy. Perhaps, as I did, you believe that only certain cigarettes taste good, like the one after a meal. If this was so, then why smoke the others? Anyway, how can two cigarettes from the same pack taste different?

Don't take my word for it; see for yourself. Smoke a cigarette consciously after a meal to see if it tastes different to the others. The reason that the smoker perceives that the one after a meal or at a social occasion is more enjoyable, is because at such times we are enjoying ourselves anyway, whether we're a smoker or a non-smoker. The one after the meal is for some people the most precious of the lot. This is because in addition to being at a time when we're having fun anyway, it also comes after a period of abstinence.

It is such a shame that smokers so value the one after a meal when the truth is that they should be acknowledging that it is the need to smoke that has ruined the meal in the first place.

As I have said many times: it's not that we enjoy smoking, it's that we're miserable when we can't smoke. But non-smokers don't get miserable when they can't smoke. The cigarette causes the misery. Why can't we see this when it is so obvious to everyone else?

Cutting down not only doesn't work, but it is also the worst form of torture. It doesn't work because smoking is not a habit, it is an addiction. You can't become less addicted to something, you're either addicted or you are not. We can't break a pack-a-day addiction and re-make it as a two-a-day addiction. You aren't deciding how much you will smoke; the rate at which your body metabolizes nicotine dictates how much you will smoke.

When we cut down, our psychological 'need' to smoke remains the same but we are only servicing that need on a limited basis. This means that we have to spend large amounts of time wanting to smoke but not allowing ourselves to do so. This builds a feeling of deprivation and sacrifice identical to that experienced by the smoker trying to quit using willpower. Therefore when we are cutting down, we have to suffer the misery of the willpower quitter without even getting the benefit of being smoke-free! It is truly the worst of both worlds. You have to apply willpower and discipline for the rest of your life. Who could think of a more miserable future?

As I said, the main problem with stopping is not the chemical aspect, but the mistaken belief that the cigarette gives you some pleasure and that as a non-smoker you will be depriving yourself of that pleasure. This mistaken belief is triggered by the brainwashing we are subjected to before we become smokers, and is reinforced by the chemical addiction once we do. All cutting down does is to reinforce this fallacy further to the extent that smoking comes to dominate the smoker's life and convince him that the most precious thing on the planet is the next cigarette.

As I've already said, it doesn't work anyway. It takes enormous amounts of willpower to cut down. If you haven't had the willpower to quit, why do you think you'll have the much larger amount of willpower needed to cut down?

Through all the smokers and ex-smokers I have met, I have heard of literally tens of thousands of attempts to quit by cutting down. I have only heard of a handful of successes. Of all the quit smoking techniques this has to be the least successful and the most unpleasant.

However, the experience of cutting down does help us to explode one of the myths about smoking because it clearly illustrates that smoking is only 'pleasurable' after a period of abstinence. It becomes very obvious that we are not enjoying the cigarette itself, but the ending of the state of misery of needing it.

So, your choices are simple:

1. Cut down for life. This is self-imposed torture and you will fail (as have hundreds of thousands of smokers before you) because smoking isn't a habit you can break and re-make in another form, but drug addiction.
2. Continue to smoke as you do now, being dominated by fear, misery and slavery
3. Break free, take your life back and give yourself the gifts of health, happiness, life and freedom

The other important point that cutting down demonstrates is that there is no such thing as one cigarette. Smoking is a chain reaction. Every cigarette creates the 'need' to smoke the next. You can't break the chain by cutting down, only by breaking the chain!

REMEMBER: CUTTING DOWN WILL DRAG YOU DOWN.

Chapter 24

Just One Cigarette

"Just one cigarette' is a myth that you must see for what it really is – a particularly cruel fantasy.

'Just one cigarette' got you hooked in the first place. Your first cigarette led to the tens of thousands of cigarettes you have had to smoke since.

'Just one cigarette' to tide us over a difficult period or on a special occasion is the cause of failure of most of our attempts to stop.

It is 'just one cigarette' that, when smokers think they are free, sends then back into the trap. Sometimes it's just to confirm that we have indeed broken free. Before you know it, you're back buying cigarettes and wondering what on earth happened. It tastes horrible and you question how you could have become hooked in the first place. You are convinced you could never get hooked again, but you already are.

It is the thought of that one 'special' cigarette that prevents smokers from trying to stop. The first one in the morning or the one after a meal.

Get it firmly into your mind: there is no such thing as 'one cigarette'. It is a chain reaction that will dominate you for the rest of your life unless you choose to break it.

It is the myth of the occasional or 'special' cigarette that keeps willpower quitters mourning the loss of their 'friend' instead of celebrating the death of an enemy. You must train yourself to see smoking for what it really is. That 'just one cigarette' led to the years and years of slavery and torture you have had to endure as a smoker. Whenever you think about smoking you must see it as a lifetime's chain of filth, disease, fear, misery and slavery. These are the facts of smoking. A lifetime of paying an exorbitant amount of money for the privilege of feeding yourself poison. A lifetime of shame, anger, guilt, bad breath and of mental and physical torture. And for what do we put ourselves through this awful experience? So we can remove the slightly empty feeling of withdrawal caused by the previous cigarette, and feel like a non-smoker.

There are two things that really grind us down about smoking. First, it's so unremitting. The cigarette has got you by the throat and, so long as you remain a smoker, it never lets go. You never get a day off, or even a couple of hours off. It doesn't matter if it's twenty below outside, or if you have a cough or a cold, or if you're on a plane or at the movies – it never lets up and gives you a break. The second thing is that it's so unrewarding. It's only when we are not smoking that the cigarette seems desirable. When we're smoking we're mostly either unaware of it or we are aware but wishing we didn't have to. All the cigarette does is remove the need to smoke and in doing so, momentarily lets you feel like a non-smoker. It is so obvious that we don't get any pleasure from it, we just feel deprived when we can't smoke. Why can't we see that it is the cigarette that is causing this unhappiness? Non-smokers don't get miserable when they can't smoke.

If you struggle with this, ask yourself a simple question. If you could go back in time to when you smoked your first cigarette, but this time you had the knowledge and experience of smoking that you have now, would you still light that cigarette? Every smoker on the planet would answer the same: "You have got to be joking!' Yet every smoker has this choice every day of his smoking life. Why don't we opt for what we know to be the smart – no, the only – choice? The answer is fear. The fear that we will be unable to enjoy life or cope with stress. What smokers don't see is that we are not enjoying life as a smoker and that the cigarette itself is causing the stress.

Stop selling yourself short. You can do this. Any smoker can. It's ridiculously easy.

In order to find it easy to stop there are a couple of fundamentals you have to get clear in your mind. We've dealt with three of them up to now:

1. There is nothing to give up. On the contrary you are giving yourself the wonderful gifts of health, happiness and freedom when you break free from the slavery of smoking.
2. There is no such thing as one cigarette; just a lifetime's chain of filth, disease and misery. Your first cigarette led to every single cigarette you have ever smoked in your life.
3. In a smoking context, there is nothing different or unique about you. All smokers are the same. All can find it easy to quit if they have the right information and the right frame of mind.

Many people believe that they are confirmed smokers or have addictive personalities. There is no such thing. No one needed to smoke before they lit that first cigarette and became hooked. It is the effect of all drugs to make us feel powerless and helpless. This makes us want the drug more so that we can remove the feeling and once again feel normal. It is the drug that addicts us, not our personalities.

These feelings of frailty and that we are somehow flawed and incomplete are promoted aggressively by advertisers in a wide range of categories, who use these fears to sell their products.

It is essential to remove this belief that we are helplessly dependent on nicotine (or any other drug for that matter). The reason for this is that if we believe it, it becomes our reality. Up to now we have believed ourselves to be dependent on cigarettes but the truth is that it is the cigarette itself that creates the 'need' to smoke. Non-smokers don't have it.

If we can replace the fear with facts, we can see the cigarette for what it really is – a nicotine delivery device – and remove the belief that we 'need' to smoke. With no 'need' to smoke or desire to do so, it's easy to break free. It is essential to remove all the brainwashing.

Chapter 25

Casual Smokers, Teenagers and Non-smokers

Heavy smokers tend to envy casual smokers. We've all met these characters: "Oh, I can go all week without a cigarette and it doesn't bother me." We think, "I wish I was like that!"

I know this is hard to believe, but there is no such thing as a happy smoker, casual or otherwise. No smoker enjoys being a smoker, which explains why so many want to quit. Never forget:

- No smoker decided that they were going to be smokers for the rest of their lives. They fell into a trap
- Some smokers find this hard to acknowledge because to do so would be to admit a flaw or weakness, so they are in denial
- They lie to themselves and others about their smoking in an attempt to justify what they know to be unjustifiable

I used to be a fanatical golfer. Because I enjoyed it so much I would play whenever I could. If casual smokers think that smoking is so enjoyable, why don't they do it more?

And why do casual smokers feel bound to say things like "I could go all week without a smoke and it wouldn't bother me." Why bother to say such a thing? If I said: "I could go a whole week without a carrot" would you think that I didn't have a problem with carrots? Or would you wonder why I was telling you this, unless I had a problem with carrots? It doesn't add up.

The casual smoker is trying to convince himself and you that he doesn't have a problem. But if he didn't have a problem, surely he wouldn't have a need to mention it? After all, I'm sure you don't go around telling people that you can go all week without shooting up with heroin. Why make such a statement unless you are a heroin addict? Only a heroin addict would be proud of going all week without.

It doesn't make sense. Casual smokers would have you believe that they could take or leave cigarettes. But if this were true, why would they take them? Which adult, knowing what we know now about smoking, would choose to become a smoker? Would you?

Actually, many casual smokers are more firmly hooked than heavy smokers. The reason for this is that they suffer from the illusion that they enjoy smoking, whereas few heavy smokers believe they enjoy smoking – they are just doing it because they don't think they can stop.

Remember, the only 'pleasure' that smokers get is the illusory one of temporarily relieving the very slight withdrawal symptoms caused by the previous cigarette. Picture that little nicotine monster as an itch. For the most part, it is so slight we are barely even aware of it.

All smokers, casual or otherwise, have this 'itch' and of course the natural tendency is to scratch it as soon as you become aware of it. By lighting up, we scratch the itch, but because our bodies build immunity to the effect of the drug, as time goes on we tend to need to smoke more to relieve it. Soon, nicotine withdrawal creates a permanent itch, and this is why most smokers become regular smokers, and also why some become chain smokers.

Casual smokers remain so for a variety of reasons:

- FEAR: They are terrified of the consequences of smoking more and think that by limiting their intake they are limiting their risk
- MONEY: They physically can't afford to smoke more, or resent paying for something they don't enjoy, so they limit their intake in an attempt to control the cost
- LACK OF OPPORTUNITY: These days many people won't smoke in their car, at work, at home or when their kids are around. This only leaves a very limited number of opportunities to smoke and so these smokers have to use significant amounts of willpower not to smoke more
- FEAR OF LOSS OF CONTROL: These people hate smoking and being a smoker. They live in fear of becoming hooked, but of course, already are

I used to think of my chain-smoking as a weakness. I couldn't understand why my friends could limit their intake to ten or twenty a day. I knew I was a very strong willed person. It never even occurred to me that most people are physically incapable of chain smoking. The truth is that these five-a-day smokers whom I envied throughout my smoking life don't smoke more because their bodies can't hack it, they detest it, they can't afford to, they are using willpower not to or they are terrified of the consequences.

Let's take a closer look at the different categories of casual smoker.

THE BEGINNER. This is the teenager who is trying the odd cigarette at parties or when hanging out with their friends. At this stage, the cigarette tastes absolutely disgusting and the teenager is convinced that he could never get hooked. Unfortunately this is exactly how and when over 95% of us became addicted and we spend the rest of our lives paying for it and trying to break free.

THE RELAPSER. This is a smoker who was previously a heavier smoker but feels he can't do without altogether. These usually fall into a couple of categories:

The Five-a-Day smoker: I envied these people my whole smoking life. It never occurred to me how unhappy they were. If they enjoy smoking, why not smoke more? If they don't enjoy it, then why smoke at all? This smoker is relieving the withdrawal pangs for less than an hour a day. For the rest of the day he is in withdrawal and having to use willpower not to scratch the itch.

The Morning-only or Evening-only smoker: He punishes himself by suffering withdrawal and using willpower for half the day so that he can relieve them for the other half. This is like banging your head against a brick wall because it feels better when you stop.

The Six-Months on, Six-Months off smoker: (Or the "I can stop whenever I want" smoker). If he enjoys smoking, then why does he want to stop? If he doesn't enjoy it, why does he start again? The truth is that this smoker is hooked 12 months of the year. When he smokes he feels lethargic and trapped and after six months he feels so bad that he needs to stop. As a non-smoker, he feels much better but over time forgets what it felt like to have to be a smoker and, because he has never dealt with the brainwashing, senses that he is depriving himself or missing out on something. So he lights a cigarette. It's pretty disgusting so he falls for the same trap as the teenager ("I could never get hooked on something as disgusting as this!"). Before he knows it, he is buying cigarettes again and the whole cycle repeats. Many smokers envy these smokers, but in many ways they are the saddest of all. When they are smokers they wish they were non-smokers and when they are non-smokers they are wishing they could smoke.

The 'I only smoke on Special Occasions' smoker: Isn't it amazing how everything seems to be a special occasion?

The *'I've stopped but just have the Occasional Cigar / Cigarette' Smoker:* This goes back to the 'just one cigarette' argument. These smokers are headed back to full-time smoking. Think about it this way: if a recovering alcoholic came to your house and said that he was 'just going to have one drink' what would you advise? Nicotine is many, many times more addictive than alcohol.

There are two other types of casual smoker. The first is the type who very occasionally smokes a cigar or cigarette, almost always at a social event. These people are really non-smokers but sense that they might be missing out on something. It's clear that they are hating every second of it. They often don't inhale and look awkward or uncomfortable when they are smoking. They just don't get smoking and can't believe that the smoker isn't enjoying it. If they are adults, they often just give up trying to enjoy it and the whole world of smoking remains an inexplicable mystery to them. If they are teenagers, many of them will persist with smoking in the mistaken belief that there must be something to it, and that they could never get hooked anyway. We all started this way.

The second category is very rare indeed. In fact, out of the tens of thousands of smokers I have personally helped, I can only think of perhaps ten or twelve such people. The type can best be described by outlining a recent case.

A woman 'phoned the clinic and insisted on talking to me personally. She was seeking a private session. She is a solicitor, had been smoking for around twelve years and during that time had never smoked more or less than two cigarettes a day. She was, it was clear, a very intelligent and strong-willed lady. I explained that the success rates at our group sessions are just as high as the private sessions, and in any event I was only able to do individual sessions if someone was so famous that their presence would disrupt the rest of the group. She began to cry and I couldn't resist the tears.

The session was expensive. Actually, most smokers would wonder why she even wanted to stop in the first place. They would gladly pay me double what that lady did in order to only smoke two cigarettes a day! However, in doing so they would be making the mistake of assuming that the lady was happy and in control. In this woman's case both her parents had died from lung cancer before she herself had started smoking. Like me, she had a terrible fear of smoking before she started. Like me, she eventually caved in under the massive brainwashing and tried her first cigarette. Like me, she can remember the foul taste. Unlike me, who capitulated and became a chain-smoker very quickly, she resisted the slide.

All you ever 'enjoy' in a cigarette is the ending of the state of 'needing' it. This is irrespective of whether or not it is the barely perceptible physical itch, or the much greater psychological torture of not being able to scratch it. Cigarettes themselves are filth and poison. This is why we only have the illusion of enjoyment after a period of abstinence. Just like thirst or hunger, the longer you experience it the greater the sense of relief.

Smokers make the mistake of believing that smoking is a habit. They think that if they can reduce their intake and maintain it, then they can break their old habit and replace it with a new one. Smoking is not a habit; it's drug addiction.

When you have an itch, the natural tendency is to scratch it. With cigarettes, as your body creates immunity to nicotine over the years, you need to smoke more to relieve the 'itch'. The more you smoke, the less effect each cigarette has, and the more you need to smoke. As the drug begins to destroy you physically and mentally, as it gradually eats away at your nervous system and your confidence and courage, you are increasingly unable to limit the interval between each cigarette. This explains why people like me, who never even have any illusion that they enjoy smoking, end up as chain-smokers, even though you hate it and every cigarette is hateful.

Back to the woman solicitor: ironically, most smokers would envy her and would be staggered to hear the misery that this poor woman had to endure. When you only smoke one cigarette every twelve hours, it appears to be the most precious thing on earth. For twelve years that poor woman was at the center of a tug-of-war. She had been unable to stop smoking but was terrified of getting lung cancer like her parents. For twenty-three hours and fifty minutes a day, she had to use willpower to fight the temptation to smoke. For the ten minutes of the day she was smoking, she felt guilt, fear, self-loathing, anger and frustration. This is not a life; it is a nightmare.

It reduced her to a wreck in the end. Just think about it logically: either there is a genuine pleasure or crutch in smoking or there isn't. If there is, who wants to wait an hour, or a day, or a week? Why should you be denied this pleasure or crutch in the meantime? If there is no genuine pleasure or crutch, why bother to smoke at all?

I remember another case, the man who was the inspiration for this book, who was a five-a-day smoker. He called me and started to talk in a croaky voice that I know to be the voice of a throat cancer victim. He said: "Mr. Carr, I just want to stop smoking before I die." This is how he described his life.

"I am sixty-one years old. I have cancer of the throat through smoking. Now I can only physically cope with five roll-ups a day.

"I used to sleep soundly through the night. Now I wake every hour and all I can think about is smoking. Even when I'm sleeping, I'm dreaming about cigarettes.

"I cannot smoke my first cigarette until ten o'clock. I get up at five o'clock and make endless cups of tea. My wife gets up at eight o'clock and because I'm so bad-tempered, she won't have me in the house. So I go down to the greenhouse and try to distract myself by pottering around, but my mind is obsessed with smoking. At nine o'clock I begin to roll my first cigarette and I do so until it's perfect. It's not that I need it to be perfect, but it gives me something to do. I then wait for ten o'clock. When it arrives my hands are shaking uncontrollably. But I don't light the cigarette then. If I do, I need to wait another three hours for the next one. Eventually I light the cigarette, take one drag and put it out. By doing this I can make the cigarette last an hour. I smoke it right down to the end, burning my fingers, lips and tongue. I put it out, then wait for the next one."

Reading this you probably have visions of some pathetic, weak-willed jellyfish of a man. Not so. He was a tall, powerful man, a decorated ex-Marine and former athlete. He didn't want to become a smoker. However, in World War II, cigarettes were provided free of charge as part of every soldier's rations. This man was virtually ordered to become a smoker and he has spent the rest of his life paying. By the time he contacted me he was a mental, physical and nervous wreck, all due to smoking and the stranglehold the cigarette had on this tragic hero's life. Had he been an animal, our society would have had him put down as a mercy killing.

So much for 'happy casual smokers.'

You may think that I am exaggerating. These cases are unusual but by no means unique. There are thousands of similar stories. That man poured his heart out to me, but you can be sure that many of his friends and acquaintances envied him for being a five-a-day man.

Isn't it strange that, as a smoker, we equate smoking less with being happier, yet we perceive not smoking at all as terrifying? It doesn't seem to occur to us that using this analysis the obvious conclusion is that the cigarette creates the misery in the first place. It also eludes us that using this rationale, the happiest people would be non-smokers. These things are very obvious to non-smokers but fear prevents smokers from accepting them.

The truth is that casual smokers are no happier than heavy smokers, and many of them are extremely unhappy indeed. The manifestation of their addiction is a little different to that of the regular smoker, but they are addicted nonetheless. As casual smokers they suffer from two additional burdens that make their lives even more miserable. Firstly, they are only servicing their addiction on a limited basis. This means that they have to use willpower and go through extended periods of enduring the torture of wanting to smoke but not allowing themselves to do so. Second, because they are abstaining on a prolonged basis, they suffer from the illusion that they enjoy smoking where in fact they are enjoying an end to the dissatisfied state of needing to smoke.

In any case, drug addicts are notorious liars and this includes all smokers. Most casual smokers smoke far more and far more frequently than they care to admit. I have lost count of the number of conversations I have had with so-called five-a-day smokers who have smoked more than five during the course of the conversation! Observe casual smokers at social occasions such as weddings and parties. They'll be chain-smoking along with the best of them.

You don't need to envy casual smokers. The truth is that they, along with all of the other smokers in your life, will be envying you when you break free. Life is so much sweeter without dragging this ball and chain with you wherever you go.

Teenagers can be more of a challenge to cure because they don't believe that they are hooked and they think they could quit anytime they wanted to. By the time they work it all out; it's too late.

I'd like to warn the parents of children who loathe smoking not to have a false sense of security. All children hate smoking right up until the time they become hooked.

It saddens and angers me that society has not found an effective way to prevent children from starting to smoke. Frankly, it's unforgivable. Health warnings don't deter them because teenagers don't think they are applicable to them. I heard that kids in Manitoba trade the cigarette warnings on packs like they're baseball cards. They treat the anti-smoking education programmes like DARE (Drug Abuse Resistance Education) as a joke. Attempts by the establishment to deter kids from smoking only serve to make it appear more desirable. The reason for this is that the children are receiving mixed messages. On the one hand, very un-cool people (teachers, doctors, health educators) are telling them that it is not cool to smoke. But on the other hand, very cool people (peers, older kids, movie stars, rock stars) are telling them that it is very cool to smoke. Put yourself in a thirteen year-olds' place, which one would you buy?

What I find genuinely difficult to accept is that we let it happen. According to the Smoke Free Movies website, between May 2002 and April 2003, 82% of top grossing PG-13 films featured smoking scenes and half of all the smoking shots were in movies rated for kids. This is up substantially from 1999-2000, when only 21% of the tobacco shots were in G, PG, and PG13 films. People tend to be shocked and horrified at such data, but there's nothing really new here. Hollywood has always been a key channel for the promotion of the smoking message, going back to the days of Dietrich, Bogart and Spencer Tracy.

I find it deeply troubling and have given much thought to this problem. I have written a book specifically addressing the issue of teenagers and prevention. I also offer advice on how to help your child break free if they have already become hooked. If you have children and are anxious that they do not become brainwashed as you were, then you should consider getting a copy. Feel free to contact your nearest Allen Carr clinic for more information.

It is an irrefutable fact that the vast majority of youngsters who end up addicted to cocaine, heroin or any other of the so-called hard drugs, are introduced to the concept of addiction by smoking tobacco. I have yet to meet a heroin addict who was not first a smoker. If you can help your children to avoid the smoking trap, you substantially reduce the risk of them becoming dependent on heavier drugs. I beg you not to be complacent in this matter. It is essential to protect youngsters at the earliest possible age and if you have a child I strongly urge you to read that book.

Chapter 26

The Secret Smoker

The secret smoker should be grouped with casual smokers, but the effects of secret smoking are so insidious that it merits a separate chapter. It can and does lead to the destruction of personal relationships and in my case, nearly caused a divorce.

I was three weeks into one of my failed attempts to stop. The attempt had been triggered off by my wife's worry about my constant wheezing and coughing. I told her that I wasn't worried about my health. She said: "I know you aren't. But how would you feel if you had to watch someone you love systematically destroying themselves?" It was an argument I found irresistible, hence the attempt to stop. The attempt ended after three weeks after a heated argument with an old friend. It did not register until years after that my devious mind had created the argument. I had never argued with this friend previously, nor have I since. This was clearly the big monster at work. Anyway, I had my excuse, lit up and was now smoking again.

I could not bear to think of the disappointment this would cause my wife, so I didn't tell her. I just smoked when alone. Then gradually I started smoking in the company of friends, until it got to the point where everyone knew I was smoking except my wife. I remember being quite pleased at the time. I thought, 'Well, at least it's cutting my consumption down.' Eventually, she accused me of continuing to smoke. I hadn't realized it, but she described the times I had caused an argument and stormed out of the house. At other times I had taken two hours to buy some minor item, and on occasions when I would normally have invited her to join me, I had made feeble excuses to go alone.

As the anti-social split between smokers and non-smokers widens, there are literally thousands of cases where the company of friends or relatives is limited or avoided altogether because of this dreadful weed. The worst thing about secret smoking is that it reinforces the fallacy in the smoker's mind that he is being deprived. At the same time, it causes a major loss of self-respect as otherwise honest and decent people are forced to deceive those whom they love most.

I remember the 1970s detective show, *Columbo*. The theme of each episode is similar. The villain, usually a wealthy and respected businessman, has committed what he thinks is the perfect murder and his confidence in remaining undetected as the perpetrator receives a boost when the shabby-looking and seemingly disorganized Columbo is assigned to the case.

Columbo has this frustrating practice of closing the door after finishing his interrogation, having assured the suspect that he is in the clear, and before the satisfied smirk has left the murderer's face, Columbo reappears with: "Just one small point sir, which I'm sure you can explain..." The suspect stammers and from that point on, he knows and we know that Columbo will gradually wear him down.

No matter how awful the crime, from that point on my sympathies were with the murderer. As a secret smoker, I felt like a criminal. The endless hours of not being able to smoke, then sneaking out into the garage for a desperation drag or two, shivering in the cold wondering where the pleasure was. The fear of being caught red-handed, like a naughty schoolboy rather than a forty year-old professional accountant and senior executive. Would she discover where I had hidden the cigarettes, lighter and butts? The relief of returning to the house undiscovered only to begin to panic about whether she would smell the smoke on my breath or clothes. As I took longer and more frequent absences so the risk increased. I knew that it was only a matter of time until I was discovered. The final humiliation and shame almost came as a relief as the sheer torture of being a secret smoker was replaced by the very slightly more tolerable torture of once again becoming a chain-smoker.

OH THE JOYS OF BEING A SMOKER!

Chapter 27

A Social Habit?

The main reason why there are now more ex-smokers in Canada than smokers is the social revolution that is taking place now with respect to smoking.

Yes, I know: health and money are the main reasons that smokers quote as the motivation to quit, but this has always been the case and doesn't totally explain the rapid decline in smoking rates. Smokers have lived with the health risks for decades. You don't need cancer scares or health warnings to know that cigarettes ruin your life. These bodies of ours are the most sophisticated machines on the planet and it tells us – no, it practically yells at us – from the first drag to the last that cigarettes are POISON.

The only reason we get dragged into it in the first place is because of the social pressure from our friends or siblings. Smoking was once considered to be a social lubricant and, to a degree, it still is by teenagers, mainly for the reasons explained in Chapter 25. But today, even most smokers acknowledge that smoking is anti-social.

When I was a smoker you could still light up in most places including offices, trains, pubs, clubs, cinemas and even friend's houses. In those days the cigarette was the proud badge of the tough guy and the sophisticated lady.

Today the situation couldn't be more different. Everyone knows that the only reason that smokers smoke is because they have failed to stop or they are too frightened to even try. Increasingly the smoker is marginalized and demonized by society. Apart from glass-walled 'Smoking Rooms' designed to humiliate the smoker and put him on display like a circus attraction, there are few indoor places for smokers to smoke. Even bars are choosing or being forced to go smoke-free. Smokers are sent outside in the wind and the rain and bitter cold. It's a lifetime of being despised by society and of despising yourself. A traumatized woman called to book into our Vancouver clinic because someone had actually spat on her when she lit up while standing on a pavement. A Toronto woman – a beautiful, classy and elegant woman in her fifties, called to make a reservation after she had been asked to smoke in the alley behind a restaurant where she was eating, along with the garbage cans and the rats.

This revolution is changing the way society looks at smokers and the way smokers see themselves. I've recently seen situations that I remember as a boy but I haven't seen for years – like smokers flicking ash into their cupped hand or even their pocket because they are too embarrassed to ask for an ashtray.

I was in a restaurant a few years ago. It was midnight and everyone had long since stopped eating. At a time when the cigarettes and cigars are usually rife, not one person was smoking. I assumed that it must be a non-smoking restaurant but when I asked the waiter he said that they had no smoking restriction. Just as we were talking, someone lit up. That plume of smoke triggered a sequence of beacons through the restaurant. All the smokers had been sitting there thinking, 'Surely I can't be the only smoker', suffering in silence and too ashamed to light up.

What was once a social habit has become a source of shame and embarrassment. And it's not getting better. Though it's difficult to imagine, things will continue to get worse for smokers in Canada. There isn't a city or town that doesn't have draconian smoking by-laws or plans to implement them. There is even talk of legislation to attempt to ban smoking in private homes and cars if ever there is the prospect of a non-smoker entering your car or home.

Every day more and more smokers leave this sinking ship. In a poll conducted for Statistics Canada over 80% of adult smokers want to quit, and this number rises to over 90% when we look at the 35 plus age group. As smokers give up in their droves, those left in the trap begin to worry about being left on their own.

DON'T LET IT BE YOU!

Chapter 28

Timing

Apart from the obvious point that, as it is doing you no good, now is the best time to stop, I believe timing to be one of the most important aspects to quitting.

Our society, despite its professed hatred of smoking, doesn't take it all that seriously. Society tends to treat smoking as a slightly distasteful habit that has unfortunate side effects with respect to health. This is a bit like saying that Wayne Gretzky could play hockey – something of an understatement. Over 1 billion people (including over 60 million North Americans) are addicted to nicotine. Smoking kills around 6 million people every year, including over 500,000 North Americans. It is, by far, the leading cause of preventable death in every developed country in the world. For many smokers, their one biggest regret in life was lighting their first cigarette.

A glance at the above is ample demonstration, if any were needed, that the stakes are very high. Your health, happiness and freedom are at stake. If you don't get this right, you could pay with your life, as those six million smokers did last year, and six million more will next year. It is important to do everything you can to give yourself the best possible chance of success and this means getting the timing right.

First of all, identify the times or occasions when smoking appears to be important to you. If you are a businessman and smoke for the illusion of stress relief, choose a relatively slack time, or perhaps your annual vacation. If you smoke mainly when you are bored, choose a time when you know you'll be busy.

Look ahead a few weeks into the future and try to anticipate whether there might be an occasion or event that might cause you to fail. Occasions like weddings or Christmas need not deter you, so long as you anticipate them in advance and do not feel you will be deprived. Do NOT attempt to cut down in the meantime, as this will only create the illusion that the cigarette is enjoyable, as explained in Chapter 23. If anything, it helps to force as many of the filthy things down you as possible. This removes even the illusion of pleasure. While you are smoking your last cigarettes be aware of the disgusting smell and taste and think how wonderful it will be when finally you allow yourself to stop doing it.

WHATEVER YOU DO, DON'T FALL INTO THE TRAP OF PROCRASTINATING AND PUTTING IT OUT OF YOUR MIND. FINALISE YOUR TIMETABLE NOW AND LOOK FORWARD TO IT. Remember, you aren't giving anything up. On the contrary, you are about to receive marvelous positive gains.

For years I've been saying that I know more about the mysteries of quitting smoking than anyone else on the planet. The problem is this: although every smoker smokes purely to relieve the chemical withdrawal created by the previous cigarette, it is not the nicotine addiction itself that hooks the smoker but the brainwashing that results from that addiction. Every individual smoker has his or her own individualized version of the brainwashing. In most aspects of the smoking conundrum these differences don't matter but in the area of timing they can be critical.

With the benefit of many years of feedback that I have received since the original publication of this book and bearing in mind that each day I learn something new about smoking, I was agreeably surprised to realize that the philosophy I propounded in the first edition was still sound. I know for a fact that every smoker can find it not only easy to stop but can actually enjoy the process. Unfortunately, knowing this is useless unless I can communicate it to smokers. And unless I can make them believe it, they will continue to believe that quitting has to be tough and unpleasant.

Many people have said to me, "You say, 'Continue to smoke until you have finished the book.' This makes people read the book slowly or just not finish it at all. Therefore you should change that instruction." This sounds logical, but I know that if the instruction were 'Stop Immediately!', some smokers wouldn't even start reading the book.

I had a smoker consult me in the early days. He said, "I really resent having to seek your help. I know I am strong-willed. I am in control of every other area of my life. Why is it that all these other smokers are stopping by using just their own willpower, yet I have to come to you?" He continued, "I think I could do it on my own, if I could smoke while I was doing it."

This may sound like a contradiction, but I knew what the man meant. We think of stopping smoking as something that is difficult to achieve. What do we need when we have a difficult or unpleasant task? We need our little 'friend'. So stopping smoking seems to the smoker to be a double blow. Not only do we have something we perceive to be difficult and unpleasant to do, but we also have to do without our crutch while we're doing it.

It didn't occur to me until long after the man had left that my instruction to keep smoking is the real beauty of the Easy Method. You can continue to smoke while you go through the process of stopping. You can get rid of all of your doubts and fears first, and when it is time to put out your last cigarette you are already a non-smoker, and a happy one!

The only chapter that has caused me to question my original advice seriously is this chapter on the matter of the right timing. Above I advise that if your special cigarette occasions are stress situations at the office, then pick a holiday to make an attempt and vice-versa. In fact, that isn't the easiest way to do it. The easiest way is pick what you feel to be the most *difficult* time to do it. In this way you can prove to yourself that you can handle even the toughest situations as a non-smoker and the rest becomes even easier. But if I gave you that as a definite instruction, would you even make the attempt to stop?

Let me use an analogy. My wife and I mean to go swimming together. Whilst we arrive at the pool at the same time, we are rarely in the water together. The reason for this is that my wife enters the water extremely slowly, dipping one toe in, then another, and so on. For me, even watching this is excruciating. I know that no matter how cold the water is, eventually I'm going to have to brave it. So I've learned to do it the easy way: I dive straight in. If I were in a position to insist that my wife either did as I did (i.e. dive straight in) or not swim at all, I know that she'd choose not to swim at all. You see the problem.

From feedback I know that many smokers have used the original advice I gave on timing to delay what they perceive to be the evil day. My next thought was to use a technique like the one I used for Chapter 21, The Advantages of Being a Smoker. It would be something like, 'Timing is very important, and in the next chapter I will advise you about the best time for you to make the attempt.' You would turn over the page and there would be a huge 'NOW!' That is in fact the best advice, but would you take it?

This is the most subtle aspect of the smoking trap. It's designed to hold you forever. When we have stress in our lives, it's not time to stop. When we have none, we have no desire to stop.

Ask yourself the following questions.

When you smoked your first cigarette, did you decide to smoke for the rest of your life, all day, every day, never being able to stop?

OF COURSE YOU DIDN'T!

Are you going to continue to smoke for the rest of your life, all day every day, never being able to stop?

OF COURSE YOU AREN'T!

So when will you stop? Tomorrow? Isn't that what you said yesterday? Next year? Isn't that what you said last year?

Isn't this what you have been asking yourself since you first realized you were hooked? Are you hoping that one morning you will wake up and just not want to smoke any more? Stop kidding yourself. I waited thirty-three years for it to happen to me and never did that day come. It's a fantasy. With drug addiction you get progressively more hooked, not less. You think it'll be easier tomorrow? Don't kid yourself. If you can't do it today, what makes you think you'll be able to tomorrow? Or will you wait until you get one of the killer diseases? Do you honestly think that the additional stress caused by the thought of impending death will make it easier to quit? Think about this; what would you advise your dearest friend to do in this situation? You would urge him to save his life and act immediately.

We believe that we live stressful lives. In fact, we don't. We've taken most of the genuine stress out of our lives. We have a comfortable roof over our heads. When we leave our home we aren't likely to be attacked by man-eating predators. Most of us don't have to worry about where our next meal is coming from. We have heat, light and clean water. Compare this to the life of a wild animal. Every time a rabbit comes out of its burrow it is confronted with life-threatening situations. One lapse in concentration and that rabbit could be someone or something's lunch. But the rabbit is equipped to handle this stress. It has adrenaline and other hormones – and so have we. The truth is that the most stressful periods in our lives tend to be childhood and early adolescence. The reason for this is that everything is new and everything is changing. During this most stressful period of our lives, we didn't need to smoke. We were perfectly able to cope. God, Mother Nature and four million years of natural selection have equipped us to cope with stress. I was five years old when World War II started. We were bombed out and I was separated from my parents for two years. I was billeted with people who treated me unkindly. It was an unpleasant period in my life, but I was able to cope with it. I don't believe it has left me with any permanent scars; on the contrary I think it has made me a stronger person. When I look back on my life there has only been one thing I couldn't handle and that was my slavery to that damned weed.

Twenty years ago, I thought I had all the worries in the world. I was suicidal – not in the sense that I wanted to jump off the top of a building but in the sense that I knew my smoking would soon kill me. I argued that if this was life with my crutch, life just wouldn't be worth living without it. What I didn't realize was that when you are physically and mentally depressed, everything gets you down. Now – twenty years on – I feel like a young boy again. Only one thing has made that change in my life: I'm now out of the smoking pit.

I know it's a cliché to say that, 'If you haven't got your health you haven't got anything' but it's true. I used to think that physical fitness fanatics like Gary Player were a pain. I used to claim that there was more to life than feeling fit: like booze and smokes. That's nonsense. When you are physically fit you can enjoy the highs more and cope with the lows better. We confuse responsibility with stress. Responsibility becomes stressful only if you are not strong enough to handle it. Characters like Humphrey Bogart are strong, dynamic, powerful people. What destroys them is not the stresses of life, or the pressure of their jobs, or old age, but the so-called crutches they turn to. Unfortunately these crutches can kill and sadly for him and millions like him, cigarettes did just that.

Look at it this way. You have already decided that you are not going to stay in the trap for the rest of your life. Therefore, at some time in your life, whether you are going to find it easy or difficult, you will have to go through the process of breaking free. Smoking is not a habit or a pleasure. It is a drug addiction and a disease. We have established that it will be harder tomorrow, not easier. With a disease that is getting progressively worse, the time to be rid of it is NOW – or as near to now as you can practically manage. You are about to trade in a beaten up old pick-up for a brand new Ferrari. Why wait another day?

Just think how wonderful it will be not to have your life dominated by a four-inch tube of paper with poison in it. Just think how wonderful it will be to replace a life of fear, misery, death and slavery with one of health, happiness, light, life and freedom! Why wouldn't it be easy – and fun?

Just follow all my instructions. You won't only find it easy after extinguishing the final cigarette: YOU'LL ENJOY IT!

Chapter 29

Will I Miss the Cigarette?

No! Once the little monster is dead and the chemical addiction is broken, any remaining brainwashing will vanish and you will find that you will be both physically and mentally better equipped not only to cope with the stresses and strains of life but to enjoy the good times to the fullest.

There is only one danger and that is the influence of people who are still smoking. There is a saying that, 'The grass is always greener on the other side.' And nowhere is this attitude more prevalent than in the area of smoking. Why is it the case with smoking, where the disadvantages are so enormous and the illusory advantages so slight, that ex-smokers tend to envy smokers?

With all of the brainwashing we are exposed to during our childhood and adolescence it is no surprise that we experiment with cigarettes and become hooked. But why is it that once we figure out that smoking is a game for losers and we manage to break free, do we immediately once again want to become a smoker? It is the influence of smokers.

It usually happens at a social occasion: maybe on vacation with friends. After a meal, a smoker lights up and the ex-smoker remembers that this is an occasion when previously he would have smoked. He forgets about the unbelievable disadvantages of smoking and sees the cigarette as something that would help him to really relax after a meal. This momentary sense of deprivation causes a pang. This is a very curious and entirely ridiculous scenario because what the ex-smoker should be remembering is how miserable smoking made him and how the smoker is envying him for being a non-smoker. This is much closer to the truth because, let's face it, every smoker on the planet, even with the warped, addicted, brainwashed mind suffering the delusion that he enjoys smoking, would rather be a non-smoker. So why do some ex-smokers envy smokers on such occasions? There are two reasons.

1. *'Just one cigarette.'* Remember: it doesn't exist. Stop seeing the cigarette as an isolated occasion and see it how it really is: just one more link in the endless chain of smoking. Don't envy smokers; pity them. It helps to observe smokers when they are smoking.

Notice how agitated and irritable they get when they can't smoke. Notice how quickly they smoke that cigarette, and how quickly they light the next. Notice how they are only happy when they are not aware that they're smoking and how self-conscious and apologetic they are when they are aware of it. Remember: they aren't enjoying any of them; they are merely feeding their addiction. But by feeding the addiction they are ensuring that they'll need to go on feeding it. So long as they feed it, it will never go away. In particular, remember that after that meal, that social occasion or that vacation, those poor smokers have to smoke all day, every day for the rest of their lives, never being allowed to stop, even for a day. The next morning, when they wake up with a mouth like a cesspit and a throat like sandpaper, what will be the first thing they do? That's right, light a cigarette and start the cycle all over again. That's what smoking is: a life sentence where life means a life of filth, disease, fear, misery and slavery. The next Budget Day, the next time those smokers inadvertently see the health warning, the next time they have a heart flutter or pains in their chest, the next time they're the only smoker in a group of non-smokers, the next time they are going out and feel fear and anxiety because they don't know if they'll be able to smoke, those poor smokers will have to continue this lifetime's chain of paying a fortune for the privilege of poisoning and suffocating themselves to death. It's a lifetime of mental and physical slavery and torture, of bad breath, stained teeth, a lifetime of fear and misery. And for what? Why do they live this life of slavery and pain? To remove that little empty feeling caused by withdrawing from the previous cigarette, and once again feel like a non-smoker. This is all smokers are trying to achieve; the state of peace they enjoyed before they ever lit that first cigarette. And what is the only thing preventing them from enjoying that feeling permanently? The cigarette!

2. The second reason why some ex-smokers (almost always people who have quit using willpower) have pangs on these occasions is because the smoker is doing something (i.e. smoking) and the ex-smoker is not. This can lead to a feeling of deprivation. Get it clear into your mind before you start: it is not non-smokers who are being deprived; it is smokers. Smokers are deprived of their:

   HEALTH
   ENERGY
   MONEY
   SELF-CONFIDENCE

PEACE OF MIND
COURAGE
SELF-ESTEEM
SELF-RESPECT
TRANQUILITY
FREEDOM

Get out of the habit of envying smokers and start seeing them for the sad, enslaved, pathetic creatures they really are. I know: I was the worlds' worst. That is why you are reading this book, and the ones who cannot face up to this reality, who go on kidding themselves, are the most pathetic of all.

You wouldn't envy a heroin addict. Heroin kills around 200 Canadians a year. Nicotine kills over 45,000 Canadians and an estimated 6 million worldwide. It has already killed far more people on this planet than all the wars in history combined. Like all drug addiction, yours won't get better. Each year it will get worse, just as it has already since the first time you smoked. If you don't enjoy being a smoker today, you'll enjoy it even less tomorrow. Don't envy smokers; pity them. Believe me, THEY NEED YOUR PITY.

Chapter 30

Will I Put on Weight?

This is another myth about smoking, spread mainly by people trying to quit using willpower and who substitute food for cigarettes. The withdrawal pangs from nicotine are very similar to hunger pangs, so the two are easily confused and some people might eat when they aren't really hungry. However, whereas eating can relieve a hunger pang, the withdrawal pangs from nicotine can never be satisfied so long as you remain a smoker.

As with any drug, after a while the body builds immunity and the drug ceases to relieve the symptoms that the previous dose created. As soon as we extinguish a cigarette, the nicotine begins to leave the body, so the withdrawal symptoms with their hunger-like pangs return. This is why the natural inclination is for smokers to smoke progressively more, and eventually become chain-smokers. Most smokers are prevented from becoming chain-smokers by one, or both, of two reasons:

1. ***Money*** – they can't afford to smoke more so they ration their intake
2. ***Health*** – in order to relieve the withdrawal pangs we have to ingest poison, and the body self-regulates because it can only process a finite amount of poison

The smoker is therefore left with a permanent hunger that he can never satisfy. This is why many smokers turn to over-eating, heavy drinking and even harder drugs in order to satisfy this perceived 'void'. As I mentioned in an earlier chapter, the vast majority of alcoholics are smokers. I wonder if this is really a smoking problem?

For the smoker the natural tendency is to start by substituting nicotine for food. During my own nightmare years I got to the stage where I cut out breakfast and lunch entirely. I would chain-smoke during the day. In the later years I would actually look forward to the evenings because I could stop smoking and give my poor lungs some respite from the punishment. However, I would be picking at food all evening. I thought it was hunger, but it was really withdrawal pangs from nicotine. In other words, during the day I would substitute nicotine for food and during the evenings, food for nicotine.

In those days I was thirty pounds heavier than I am today and there wasn't a thing I could do about it.

Once that little monster leaves your body, that awful feeling of insecurity leaves with it. Your confidence returns, together with a marvelous feeling of achievement and self-respect. You feel in control of your life, and you can use that control to determine not only your eating habits, but in a wide variety of wonderful ways. This is one of the many great advantages of being free from this awful weed.

As I have said, the weight myth is perpetuated by willpower quitters who substitute food for cigarettes during the withdrawal period, and then continue to overeat. Let's be clear about this: stopping smoking does not lead to weight gain; overeating does. Food and any other substitutes make it harder to quit smoking, not easier, as I shall explain in Chapter 37.

Provided you follow all the instructions, weight gain should not be a problem for you. However, if you already have a weight problem, or you want more information to give you peace of mind, I would recommend that you read *Allen Carr's EASYWEIGH to Lose Weight* which is based on the same principles as this book and makes weight control a pleasure.

Chapter 31

Avoid False Incentives

Many smokers, while trying to stop by using willpower, try to increase their levels of motivation by providing false incentives.

There are many examples of this. A typical one is 'My family and I can have a great vacation on the money I'll save.' This appears to be a logical and sensible approach, but in fact it is a false incentive because any smoker worth his salt would rather smoke fifty-two weeks a year and not have a vacation. In a way, this approach can even heighten the sense of deprivation because the smoker now perceives that he has to abstain for fifty weeks to go on a vacation that he feels that he'll never be able to enjoy without a cigarette anyway. This makes the cigarette even more precious in the smoker's mind. Instead, you should focus on the other side: What am I getting out of the cigarette? Why do I need to smoke?

Another example: 'I'll be able to afford a better car.' That's true, and the incentive may help you to abstain until you have your car, but what then? Once the novelty has gone, you once again feel deprived and sooner or later, you fall into the same trap again.

Another typical example is the office or family bet or pact. These sometimes have the advantage of helping to motivate you at certain times of the day, but they almost always end in failure. Why?

1. The incentive is false. Why should we want to stop just because other people are doing so? All this does is create additional pressure, which increases the sense of deprivation and sacrifice. If you and a group of friends, family or colleagues want to quit together, and plan on supporting each other through the process, that's great. But a pact tends to create additional pressure that can make it difficult for a group member to ask for help. This can turn participants into secret smokers, which increases the sense of deprivation and dependency even further.
2. The 'Rotten Apple' theory, or inter-dependence. With the Willpower Method of stopping, the smoker is a fragile creature undergoing a period of misery and torture while waiting for the urge to smoke to disappear. For reasons I have already discussed, using this

method one or more participants is guaranteed to fail, and this failure will come sooner rather than later. This gives the other participants the excuse they have been waiting for. With the pact broken or the bet won, the other participant(s) have no motivation to stay stopped. It's not their fault – they would have held out – it's just that Bruce or Doug or Sharon let them down. The truth is that most of them have already been cheating themselves.

3. 'Sharing the credit' is the flip side of the 'Rotten Apple' theory. It's true that the loss of face is not so bad when shared around, but who wants to fail in the first place? The problem is that if, against all the odds you are using willpower and you do succeed, you have to share the credit with the other members of the group. I'm not one to hog the limelight, but stopping smoking is a truly major event and it's only right and proper that you get all the credit that this wonderful achievement deserves.

Another classic example of false incentives is the bribe (e.g. the parent offering the teenager money to remain smoke-free or the bet 'I'll give you $100 if I fail.'). There was once an example of this in a TV programme I was watching. A policeman attempting to quit using willpower put a $50 note in his cigarette pack. He had a pact with himself. He could smoke again, but before he did so, he had to set light to the $50 bill. This stopped him for a couple of days, but eventually he burned the note. I wouldn't have lasted twenty minutes.

Stop kidding yourself. If the $300,000 the average smoker needs to spend to finance a smoking habit won't stop him, or the one-in-two risk of contracting a life-threatening disease, or a lifetime of fear, misery and mental and physical slavery, or the lifetime of humiliation and degradation being despised by society and despising yourself, then what chance does a $50 note – or any other false incentive – have?

False incentives make it harder, not easier, to stop because they focus on the illusory 'sacrifice' the smoker makes. Keep looking at the other side – the side based on facts, not fear. What is the cigarette doing for me? ABSOLUTELY NOTHING.

Why do I need to do it? YOU DON'T. YOU ARE ONLY PUNISHING YOURSELF.

Chapter 32

The Easy Way to Stop Smoking

This chapter contains instructions about the easy way to stop smoking. Providing you follow these instructions, you will find that stopping ranges from relatively easy to enjoyable.

It is ridiculously easy to stop smoking. All you have to do is two things.

1. Make the decision that you will never, ever have to smoke again
2. Don't mope about it; Celebrate.

You are probably asking, 'Why the need for the rest of the book? Why couldn't you have said that in the first place?' The answer is that at some stage you would have moped about it and consequently, you would have doubted your decision. You would have been forced to use willpower and, as a result, most likely would have failed.

As I have said before, the smoking trap is a very subtle and sinister one. The main problem in quitting is not the chemical withdrawal, this is barely even noticeable, but the brainwashing and it was therefore necessary to explode those myths and illusions. Understand your enemy. Know his tactics, and you will easily defeat him.

I spent thirty-three years trying to stop smoking the hard way and I suffered seemingly endless weeks of black depression. When I finally broke free I went from a hundred cigarettes a day to zero without a single bad moment or pang of regret. I even enjoyed the withdrawal period because I saw it for what it really was – a barely noticeable feeling in the pit of my stomach, which was a signal that the little monster was dying. The truth of the matter is that stopping smoking is the most wonderful thing that has happened in my life.

I couldn't understand why it had been so easy and it took me a long time to work it out. It was this. I knew for certain that I was never going to have to smoke ever again. During my previous attempts, no matter how determined I was, I was basically *trying* to stop smoking. I was hoping that if I could survive long enough without a cigarette, the urge would eventually go. Of course it didn't go because I was waiting for something to happen and the more I moped about it, the more I wanted a cigarette, so the craving never went.

My final attempt was different. Like all smokers nowadays, I had been giving the matter serious thought for some time. Up to then, whenever I failed, I had consoled myself with the thought that it would be easier next time. It never occurred to me that I might have to go through the rest of my life smoking. This thought filled me with horror, and started me thinking very deeply about the subject.

Instead of lighting up sub-consciously, I became more aware of my smoking and analyzed my thoughts and feelings as I was smoking. This confirmed what I already knew. I wasn't enjoying any of them and they were truly filthy, disgusting things.

I started looking at non-smokers. Until then I had always regarded non-smokers as wishy-washy, humorless, unsociable and pedantic people. However, when I looked more closely it became clear that they were stronger and far more relaxed than smokers. They appeared to be able to cope with life and handle stress and it was obvious that they were having far more fun than smokers. They had energy and a zest for life that I envied.

I started talking to ex-smokers. Up to this point I had regarded ex-smokers as people who had been forced to stop smoking for health reasons or because they could no longer afford it, but that had a secret longing to smoke. A few did say, "You get the odd pang, but it really isn't worth bothering about." But most said: "Miss it? You must be joking. I've never felt better in my life!"

Talking to ex-smokers exploded another myth I had always believed. I thought that I had some inherent weakness in me, but it suddenly dawned on me that all smokers go through this private nightmare. Basically, I said to myself, "Millions of people are stopping and are much happier now than when they were smokers. I didn't need to do this before I got started and I had to work hard to get used to the filthy things. So why do I need to do it now?" I now knew that I didn't enjoy smoking. In fact I hated the whole filthy ritual, and I did not want to spend the rest of my life being the slave of this disgusting weed.

I said to myself: "Allen, whether you like it or not, YOU HAVE SMOKED YOUR LAST CIGARETTE.'

I knew, right from that point that I would never, ever smoke again. I wasn't expecting it to be easy; in fact just the reverse. I fully believed that I was in for months of black depression and that I would spend the rest of my life having the occasional pang. Instead, it has been absolute bliss right from the start.

It took me a long time to work out why it had been so easy and why I had not suffered those terrifying withdrawal pangs that had characterized all of my previous attempts. The reason is that they only exist in the mind. They are created by doubt and uncertainty. If you remove the doubt, the 'cravings' never come.

The beautiful truth is that IT IS EASY TO STOP SMOKING. It is only the indecision and moping about it that make it difficult. Even when they are addicted to nicotine, smokers can go relatively long periods without smoking and it doesn't bother them. It's only when you want a cigarette but can't have one that the sense of deprivation comes.

Therefore the key to making it easy is to make stopping certain and final. Not to *hope* you have kicked it, but to *know* you have. Never doubt or question your decision. In fact, celebrate it.

If you can have this degree of certainty from the start, it will be easy. But how can you be certain from the start unless you know it's going to be easy? This is why the rest of the book is necessary. There are a couple of essential points that you need to be very clear about before you start,

1. Realize that you can do this. There is nothing different about you. Millions of Canadians have done it and you can too. The only person who can make you smoke that next cigarette is you.
2. There is absolutely nothing to give up. On the contrary, there are enormous positive gains to be made. I don't just mean you will be healthier and wealthier. I mean that you will enjoy the good times infinitely more (and there will be more of them) and you will be less miserable during the bad times (and there will be fewer bad times).
3. Get it clear into your head that there is no such thing as one cigarette. Smoking is a drug addiction and a chain reaction. The first cigarette you ever smoked is responsible for every cigarette you have since smoked.
4. See smoking for what it really is: it's not a slightly unpleasant habit with some unfortunate side effects; it is a drug addiction and a disease. Face up to the fact that, whether you like it or not, YOU HAVE GOT THIS DISEASE. It won't go away just because you pretend it doesn't exist. Remember, like all progressive diseases, it not only lasts for life it gets worse and worse. The easiest and best time to get rid of this disease is NOW.
5. Separate the disease (i.e. the chemical addiction) from the frame of mind of being a smoker or a non-smoker. All smokers, if given the chance to go back in time to before they got hooked, would choose to be a non-smoker. You have that opportunity today!

Embrace it. As soon as you make the decision to smoke your final cigarette you become a non-smoker. A smoker is one of those poor souls who have to go through life enslaved to a drug that doesn't even get them high – and they have to face incredible risks to their health and incredible damage to their bank balance to do it. A non-smoker doesn't. Once you have made the decision to break free from the misery and slavery of smoking, you become a non-smoker. You should celebrate right from the outset, and you should continue to celebrate for the rest of your life.

By this stage, if you have opened your mind as I asked at the beginning, you will have already decided that you are going to stop. If you have the right frame of mind, your success is guaranteed. Many readers are now feeling excitement at the prospect of their new lives and are straining at the leash to get on with it, barely able to wait to get the poison out of their system.

If you are feeling a sense of doom or gloom, it will be for one of the following reasons.

1. Something hasn't quite 'clicked'. Re-read the above five points, and ask yourself if you believe them to be true. If you doubt any of them, re-read the appropriate chapter.
2. You fear failure itself. Do not worry. Just read on. You will succeed. The whole business of smoking is like a confidence trick on a grand scale. Intelligent people do fall for con tricks, but only once. You will not fall for the same con trick again so you should have no fear of failure.
3. You agree with everything, but you are still miserable. Don't be. Open your eyes. Something marvelous is happening. You are about to escape from the prison. Anyway, the cigarette causes the misery – non-smokers aren't miserable when they can't smoke!

It is essential to start with the right frame of mind: isn't it marvelous that I am a non-smoker!

All we have to do now is to keep you in this positive frame of mind during the withdrawal period (three days), and the next few chapters deal with specific points that will enable you to do just that. By the end of the withdrawal period you will be thinking this way automatically and naturally as you begin to experience the delights of breaking free for yourself. At that stage, the only mystery in your life will be, "This is so obvious; why didn't I see it before?" However, two important warnings:

1. Delay your plan to put out your final cigarette until you have finished the book.

2. I have mentioned several times a withdrawal period of three days (after which over 99% of the nicotine has left the body) or three weeks (when there is not a single molecule of nicotine in your body). This may give the impression that it is necessary to suffer for a period. This is not the case. Physical withdrawal does exist, but it's so slight that most smokers aren't even aware of it, sleeping through the night quite happily whilst experiencing the worst period of withdrawal. You might be expecting some great cataclysmic event at three days or three weeks but it won't come. You won't suddenly feel like a non-smoker because non-smokers don't feel different to smokers. You'll feel happier, healthier and wealthier, but you will still be you. This is an important point. You become a non-smoker the second you can be happy not to have to smoke. This can happen even before you put out your final cigarette. Nicotine is a red herring. Don't focus on three days or three weeks because this gives the cigarette a hold over you during that period, a hold you have already broken by putting out your final cigarette.

Chapter 33

The Withdrawal Period

Although you are more or less nicotine-free after three days of abstinence it can take up to three weeks before our mind and body become fully accustomed to the absence of nicotine and many of the other 4,000+ chemicals present in each tobacco smoke.

During this period, you may feel 'withdrawal pangs' that consist of two very separate factors.

1. Physical withdrawal, which is a slightly empty, insecure feeling similar to hunger. If you notice it at all (and why should you? you probably didn't notice it when you were a smoker) you will find that it disappears after a maximum of three days because by this time the body has metabolized all of the nicotine. Actually, these 'pangs' are signs of your recovery and you should welcome each one.
2. The psychological trigger of certain events such as a 'phone call or a coffee break.

It is the failure of willpower quitters to understand and differentiate between these two distinct factors that make their attempts to quit so miserable and unsuccessful.

Although 'pangs' are not painful as such, it is important not to underestimate their potential influence if we approach this task with the wrong mental attitude.

If smokers using willpower to quit can manage to abstain for a few days, the physical component of the 'pang' disappears. It is the psychological triggers that cause the difficulty. That smoker has grown accustomed to relieving his need to smoke at certain times of the day and when doing certain things. Over time, these associations can become quite strong. Thus the smoker forms the view that he can't have a coffee, or drink a beer, or take a break, or enjoy a meal without a cigarette. It is important to deal with this point and best to do so by using an example.

Let's say that you have had your car for a couple of years and that the indicator lever is on the left of the steering column. You buy a brand new car and of course, the indicator is on the right. You know it's on the right, but for a couple of weeks, until you become accustomed to it, you occasionally put the windscreen wipers on whenever you want to indicate.

Stopping smoking is similar. During the early days certain events will trigger the thought 'I want a cigarette.' This is because for all of the years you were a smoker, you associated this event with smoking. In such situations, 'I want a cigarette' becomes a conditioned reflex. It is essential to counter-condition your response in these situations otherwise you will interpret your conditioned 'I want a cigarette' response as fact and then feel deprived because you can't have one. This is the beginning of the slippery slope of having to use willpower.

A common such trigger is a meal, particularly one at a restaurant with friends. The ex-smoker having to use willpower already feels depressed and deprived. When his friends light up after the meal this feeling is exacerbated. Because the brainwashing still exists, he believes that his friends are enjoying the cigarette rather than merely removing the dissatisfied state of needing a cigarette. This accentuates the feeling of deprivation further and requires the ex-smoker to apply substantial amounts of willpower to get through the occasion. The saddest thing here is that even though he is not smoking, the cigarette is still dominating the ex-smoker's life.

Even with my method, responding correctly to these triggers is the most challenging part and it can make the difference between finding stopping an OK experience and a life-changing one.

It is essential to counter this conditioning from the start and to do so successfully you must replace the fear and confusion caused by the brainwashing with hard facts. Get it clear in your mind: you don't need to smoke and you don't need to torture yourself by regarding the cigarette as some sort of crutch or friend when you know for a fact that it is neither. There is no need to be miserable. Cigarettes don't make meals or social occasions; they ruin them. Smokers aren't smoking after a meal because they enjoy it, but because they are drug addicts who need their 'fix' after a period of abstinence.

Abandon the ridiculous concept of smoking as being pleasurable for its own sake. If we smoked just for the sake of smoking, we could smoke herbal cigarettes (no, not that kind of herb!). The reason that herbal cigarettes haven't taken off here or anywhere else is that there is no point in smoking them because they haven't got any nicotine. It might help to think about it by using a comparison with heroin. Do you think a heroin addict shoots up because he enjoys using a hypodermic or to get the drug? It's so obvious with other people's addictions, isn't it? Smokers smoke to get nicotine, not because they enjoy the act of smoking. As a vivid demonstration of this, look at the story of *Next*.

Next was launched by the world's biggest tobacco company, Philip Morris, in 1989. It was touted as a nicotine-free cigarette and the nicotine was removed by using high-pressure carbon dioxide in a process similar to the method used by coffee companies when making decaffeinated coffee (they were referred to as "de-nic" cigarettes internally at Philip Morris). Smokers hated them though. After experimenting with them, it began to dawn on smokers that there is no point in smoking apart from to get the nicotine, and that there was no pleasure in the physical act of smoking for its own sake. The product flopped and was withdrawn.

Once you can see that there is no aspect of smoking that is remotely approaching pleasurable, you will have no more need to stick a cigarette in your mouth than you would in your ear.

Whether the pang is due to physical withdrawal or the psychological trigger mechanism, accept it. There is no physical pain and with the right mental approach you can brush it off as if it were a bit of fluff on your coat.

Instead of feeling fearful and anxious about pangs, embrace them. Say to yourself: 'I know what this is – it's the little nicotine monster dying. This is what smokers suffer from their whole lives and that's what keeps them smoking. Non-smokers don't get these pangs. Isn't it great that I am breaking free from this awful addiction and looking forward to a life of freedom?'

Don't focus on the pang, but on what it represents – the death not of a friend, but of a terrible enemy. One that enslaved you for years and stole your health, your money, your self-respect, your courage and confidence, all the time trying to kill you.

Think of the next few days and weeks as a game of poker where you have a Royal Flush and your opponent doesn't even have a pair of twos. You have the better cards and will crush him, so he'll try to cheat and trick you. Whatever he throws at you doesn't matter because it doesn't change the facts. You have the winning hand. You are going to win and at last be able to claim the prize you so richly deserve – a life of health, happiness and freedom.

You have him just where you want him. You have used facts to see through the confusion and fear that he has created to try to keep you trapped. As every minute passes, he becomes weaker. He will try everything. He'll try to make you miserable; he'll try to get you to call the whole thing off. But you are going to keep your eye on the prize. Nothing he does can stop you. It's over. You have won. You are free.

Whatever you do, don't try not to think about smoking. This is a tactic used by people who are quitting using willpower. They try not to think about smoking, but of course this makes them think about it even more.

Soon they are obsessed and can't get the cigarette out of their mind. You *will* think about smoking – but it's *what* you are thinking that it important. Whenever you think about smoking, think how wonderful it is that you have broken free. SAVOUR EACH THOUGHT AND EACH MOMENT. REMIND YOURSELF HOW WONDERFUL IT IS TO BE FREE ONCE AGAIN AND CELEBRATE THE PURE JOY OF NO LONGER BEING A PRISONER, A SLAVE AND AN ADDICT.

As I have said, with this mental approach, pangs that would torture a willpower quitter will become moments of pure pleasure and achievement for you. You will be amazed at how quickly smoking becomes a total non-issue in your life.

Willpower quitters frequently doubt their decision to quit because they still suffer from the illusion that they enjoyed smoking and this causes the sense of deprivation we have already discussed at some length. You, on the other hand have removed any doubts and as a result can focus on enjoying the process of breaking free and remaining a happy non-smoker.

If one of your smoking friends offers you a cigarette, you can be proud to say, "No, thanks" safe in the knowledge that he will be envying not only the fact that you are a non-smoker, but such an obviously happy one. It'll hurt him to think that one more smoker has broken out of the prison, but at the same time it'll give him hope that maybe he too can get free.

Remember that you have traded in a life of fear, misery and slavery for one of health, happiness and freedom. Remember the tens or even hundreds of thousands of dollars that one cigarette would cost you and ask yourself whether you would pay this money just to be a slave to something that you detest and will most likely kill you in the most terrible way imaginable.

Some smokers fear that they will have to go through the rest of their lives reversing these conditioned responses that smokers have in certain situations. In other words, they see themselves as having to use psychological tricks to kid themselves into believing that they don't need to smoke. This is not so. I am not asking you to use mindless optimism to drown out rational thought; I'm asking you to use rational thought to drown out fear and confusion. There is a saying that the optimist sees the bottle as half-full and the pessimist sees it as half empty. In the case of smoking, the bottle *is* empty and the smoker sees it as full. It is the smoker who has been brainwashed, not the rest of society! Once you start telling yourself that you don't need to smoke, and letting yourself be happy about not having to smoke, it's amazing how quickly this replaces the conditioned response of the brainwashed smoker. The reason that this 'takes' so easily is because it is the truth. You do not need to smoke. It's the last thing you need to do; make sure it isn't the last thing you do.

Chapter 34

Just One Drag

This is the undoing of many smokers trying to stop using willpower. They go through three or four days then have the odd couple of drags 'just to tide me over'. They have no idea of the devastating effect this has on their frame of mind.

For the vast majority, the first drag is disgusting, and this gives them a conscious boost. They think, 'Good, it wasn't enjoyable. I'm losing the urge to smoke.' The point is that CIGARETTES WERE NEVER ENJOYABLE. Enjoyment wasn't the reason you smoked, if it was, nobody would ever smoke more than one cigarette.

The only reason you smoked was to feed the little nicotine monster. You were a drug addict. Just think: you had starved him for three days and he was, to all intents and purposes, dead. Then you threw him a lifeline. How precious that one puff must have been to him! Now he's alive again, craving nicotine, and you have undone three days of work.

That drag has two damaging effects:

1. It keeps the little monster alive craving nicotine, after you had all but killed him
2. It keeps the big monster alive in your mind wanting a cigarette because you associate nicotine with cigarettes

Don't play this dangerous game. There is only one loser – you. I absolutely guarantee you that you will be back smoking regularly before you know it.

Just one cigarette is exactly how every smoker on the planet started, and it is also how every single ex-smoker on the planet relapsed.

Don't play games with yourself over something this important. If you have one drag, you will be smoking for the rest of your life.

Chapter 35

Will it be Harder for Me?

The combination of factors that will determine how easily each individual will find it to quit is infinite. To start with, each of us has our own character, personal circumstances, motivation, timing etc.

In my experience, people from certain professions tend to find it a little more difficult than others because they find it difficult to allow themselves to let go of the brainwashing.

The most obvious category is members of the medical profession. We tend to think that it should be easier for doctors to quit because they see at first hand on a daily basis the carnage that smoking causes. This, sadly, is not the case for the following reasons.

1. The constant reminder of the damage cigarettes can cause tends to be stressful. Because smokers associate stress relief with cigarettes, it tends to make them want to smoke
2. Doctors are incredibly busy people and therefore only able to smoke on a very limited basis. This has the effect of making every cigarette appear precious, and this can lead to a sense of deprivation which can make it harder to quit using willpower
3. Doctors feel tremendously guilty and, dare I say it, stupid being a smoker. This increases the pressure for them to quit and creates additional stress, which in turn makes it harder to stop using willpower

Having said that, many members of the medical profession find it ridiculously easy to quit with the Easy Method because they are smart, they understand the difference between the physical and psychological aspects of the addiction and they are aware of the power of the mind.

Other people who sometimes find it more challenging than others are people who have intense periods of activity followed by extended periods of inactivity. Car salesmen for example have a lot of 'downtime' when they are bored and they tend to smoke to provide a distraction. These long periods of relative inactivity are often followed by or sandwiched between periods of intense activity and pressure, when they smoke for the illusory 'relief' it gives them.

Homemakers are sometimes in a similar situation. No one works harder than a homemaker in my experience, but although much of the work can be stressful, it can also be boring. Long periods of monotonous housework are 'rewarded' by a cigarette, and the homemaker's day can be mapped out by limited, and therefore precious, opportunities to smoke.

The challenge for these types of individual is to see through the brainwashing of the cigarette as an all-purpose stress reliever / stimulant / relaxant / reward / comforter / friend and to see it for what it really is: a drug delivery device, much like the heroin addict's hypodermic syringe. This is easy with the right frame of mind. Believe it or not, it is not compulsory to mope around craving cigarettes when these triggers come. Instead, why not use that opportunity to celebrate your freedom and congratulate yourself that you have got rid of this evil monster?

Like I said, there is no reason on earth why these moments should not be moments of genuine pleasure. You have every reason to be thrilled with this wonderful achievement.

Remember, any smoker, regardless of age, gender, profession, intelligence and smoking history can find it easy and enjoyable to stop provided YOU FOLLOW ALL THE INSTRUCTIONS.

Chapter 36

The Main Reasons for Failure

There are two main reasons for failure with the Easy Method.

The first is the influence of other smokers. At a weak moment at a social occasion – most likely involving alcohol – someone will light up. I have already covered this topic at length. Use that opportunity to remind yourself that there is no such thing as one cigarette and that that smoker has to go on smoking all day, every day for the rest of his life, never being allowed to stop. Remember that the smoker envies you, and feel sorry for him. Believe me, he needs your pity. I wouldn't wish the life of a smoker on my worst enemy.

The other main reason for failure is just plain having a bad day. You need to get it clear in your mind that everyone has good and bad days, whether you are a smoker or a non-smoker.

The problem with the willpower quitter is that he tends to blame a bad day on the absence of the cigarette. He mopes around feeling deprived and makes a bad day worse. On the other hand the Easy Method quitter celebrates the fact that, even though today isn't good, at least he doesn't have the additional stress and misery of being a smoker on top of it.

When you are a smoker you have to block your mind to the many, many downsides of smoking. Smokers never have smoker's coughs, just permanent colds. They never have to freeze outside in the depths of a Canadian winter; they just 'go for a bit of fresh air'. As a smoker, if your car breaks down in the middle of nowhere, you light a cigarette. But does this deal with the problem? A willpower quitter in a similar situation would mope for a cigarette, as if the cigarette would solve the problem, but why? Smoking a cigarette does precisely nothing to advance or improve your predicament, so why do we attribute these magical properties to it?

This moping creates an impossible situation. You are miserable because you can't smoke, and you'll be even more miserable if you do. You know that you have made the right decision, and you have made that decision based on irrefutable facts. Every smoker on the planet would rather be a non-smoker and every non-smoker is glad they don't have to smoke. Never punish yourself by doubting this decision. It is one of the best, if not the very best decision that you have ever made.

You can be happy, not because Allen Carr tells you to be, but because there is so much to be happy about. This is a fact. As with every other area in our lives, a positive mental approach is essential – always.

Chapter 37

Substitutes

Substitutes include gum, candy, pills, patches and chocolate. DO NOT USE ANY OF THEM. They make it harder to quit, not easier because they perpetuate the myth that you have given something up and you need to replace it with something else. That quitting smoking has left a hole in your life that needs to be filled. Smoking was the hole in your life. When you get rid of the cigarette, you fill the hole and are once again complete.

Please bear the following points in mind:

1. Smoking is a disease. You do not need a replacement disease
2. You do not need nicotine. It is a poison.
3. Cigarettes create a void; they don't fill it. Non-smokers don't have this void, and they therefore don't need to look for cigarettes or any substitute to fill it.

In particular you must avoid any product that involves nicotine, whether it be gum, patch, nasal spray, inhalator or, the latest and most bizarre gimmick, nicotine water. It is true that a small proportion of smokers who attempt to quit using nicotine substitutes do succeed and attribute their success to such products. However they quit despite them, not because of them. It is sad that doctors continue to prescribe such products when they are clearly of such little help to smokers. I can't imagine that they prescribe many other treatments that have something like a 90% failure rate.

The medical community's love affair with Nicotine Replacement Therapy (NRT) is not entirely surprising though. We tend to think that there is a pill for everything these days. Actually, NRT sounds reasonable and logical. It is based on the belief that when you quit smoking, you have two powerful enemies to defeat:

1. The psychological or psycho-social triggers which make up the 'habitual' side of smoking
2. The terrible physical withdrawal from nicotine

If you have to take on two enemies, common sense would tell you that it is probably better to do it one at a time. So the theory behind NRT is to continue to take nicotine whilst you fight the psychological side of the addiction. Once this objective is achieved, we can then wean ourselves off the physical side of the addiction. In this way, you are tackling each problem separately.

The problem with this is that it is based on a flawed premise. Smoking isn't a habit, it's drug addiction and the actual physical withdrawal from nicotine is so slight as to be virtually imperceptible. Furthermore, NRT implies that smokers only go through withdrawal whenever they try to quit. In fact, smokers go through withdrawal throughout their smoking lives, and it is the desire to relieve these feelings of withdrawal that creates the perceived 'need' to smoke. As soon as the smoker extinguishes a cigarette, the nicotine begins to leave the body. Even in smokers who metabolize nicotine relatively slowly, an hour after putting out a cigarette nicotine levels have dropped to less than half. During that first hour the smoker is experiencing withdrawal at its worst because this is when the nicotine is being metabolized at the fastest rate. This is interesting, because every smoker on the planet can (and does) regularly go for an hour without smoking and it doesn't bother them in the slightest.

After six hours just under 3% of the nicotine from that cigarette remains (along with minor residual amounts from previous cigarettes). Even chain smokers can sleep six hours at night without waking to smoke. By the morning, in purely physical terms, we are virtually nicotine free. After just three days, we are nicotine free. This begs the question of why we need to use NRT for such extended periods (the patch, for example, is a ten week programme). All this does is prolong the life of the little monster and, because your brain associates nicotine with cigarettes, it keeps the big monster alive and wanting to smoke.

Think about it this way. Would you tell an alcoholic who was trying to quit to do so by drinking beer instead of wine? To stop being a nicotine addict, you must stop taking nicotine. All the people we see at our clinics who are addicted to nicotine gum remind me of this simple, unarguable truth. Don't be fooled by the fact that the gum tastes awful – so did the first cigarette, remember?

NRT also has two other important negative impacts on the psychology of the quitter.

1. In addition to keeping the little monster and the big monster alive, NRT convinces the smoker that the physical withdrawal from nicotine is so bad that he needs a patch or gum to handle it. This, because of the power of the mind, becomes a self-fulfilling prophecy. A smoker who could previously go several hours without a cigarette with no bother at all, suddenly experiences terrible

physical withdrawal just a few minutes into his quit. How can this possibly have anything to do with nicotine?

2. The use of NRT products (indeed any substitute) also perpetuates the notion that the smoker is 'giving something up' – that nicotine does something more than merely remove the symptoms of withdrawal created by the previous cigarette. This, as I have said repeatedly, leads to a sense of sacrifice, and it is this that triggers feelings of deprivation, misery and vulnerability. This necessitates the use of enormous amounts of willpower, which in turn leads to failure rates around the 90% region.

The launch of Zyban is one of the biggest and most controversial changes to the smoking cessation landscape in recent years. It has been around as an anti-depressant (Wellbutrin) for quite a while, but was repackaged as a cessation aid in the late 1990s.

I have read extensively about Zyban and spoken to hundreds of smokers who have attempted to quit by using it. I have to admit to being fairly bemused by the whole concept of it. In addition to admitting '...it is unclear exactly how Zyban works...' which I find a little alarming, the manufacturer's website states that Zyban 'reduces the urge to smoke'. But what is an 'urge', and how do you measure it? How can you scientifically measure two different 'urges' from two different people? An 'urge' isn't something uniform that you can measure like a sack of potatoes; every single one is different and every person is different. Anyway, why try to 'reduce the urge to smoke' when it's just as easy to remove it altogether?

Think of two Zyban quitters sitting having coffee. One says, "Wow! That was a huge craving. This Zyban isn't working." The other says, "I had one too. But mine was OK, this Zyban is really working!" Might it be possible that these two people had the identical feeling but that due to a million outside factors, they interpreted and processed those feelings differently? Could it be possible that one person has a lower discomfort threshold?

Isn't this really saying that the desire to smoke is mental, and that we can use the power of the mind to reduce or even eliminate the desire to smoke? This is the EASYWAY – to remove the desire to smoke. Why do we need a drug to help us do this? Why not just use an open mind and facts? Why not permanently remove our desire at a cognitive level, rather than merely temporarily suppressing it? If we are not confronting and dealing with our desire to smoke, but merely using a drug to suppress it, what happens when you stop taking the medication? Does the desire return?

Interestingly, both Zyban and NRT manufacturers advocate fairly intensive counseling as a critical element of their respective programmes (in fact, it is difficult to find published success rates for these products without the counseling element, which makes it difficult to evaluate their true efficacy).

For me, there is something counter-intuitive about treating drug addiction with drugs (particularly the drug you are trying to kick). Zyban only began to make sense to me after a conversation I had with a doctor from Vancouver who attended a clinic. He said that he prescribed Zyban to people trying to quit 'to cope with the symptoms of depression caused by quitting using willpower.' This makes perfect sense to me: he is prescribing it as an anti-depressant, which is precisely what it is. Using the EASYWAY, you don't need an anti-depressant, because there is nothing to be depressed about. On the contrary, this can and should be one of the most enjoyable experiences of your life.

As concerns other substitutes, they all have the same negative impact on quitting because they all perpetuate the myth that you have 'given something up' and that it needs to be replaced in order to 'fill the void'.

I'm now talking about the whole business of 'I can't have a cigarette so I'll have some gum/candy/chocolate to help fill the void.' Although the slightly empty feeling associated with nicotine withdrawal is similar to hunger for food, one will not satisfy the other. In fact, if there is anything designed to make you want to smoke, it's stuffing yourself with gum or mints.

But the chief downside of substitutes is that they prolong the real problem, which is the brainwashing. When you recover from a bad dose of the 'flu', do you look for a replacement? Of course you don't. By saying 'I need a substitute for smoking' you are really saying 'I am making a sacrifice'. This is the cause of the depression and misery experienced by both smokers (throughout their smoking lives whenever they are in a situation when they can't smoke) and people quitting using willpower. All substitutes do is substitute one problem for another. There is no pleasure in stuffing candy down your throat. You will just get fat and miserable, and in no time at all, you'll find yourself back on the weed, but this time twenty pounds heavier.

Casual smokers find it difficult to dismiss the belief that they are being deprived of their little reward or crutch: the cigarette during the coffee break at work or the smoke break while working in a dull or high-pressure job. Some say 'I wouldn't even take the break if I didn't smoke.' This proves my point. Often, the break is taken not because we want or need it, but so we can feed the little monster. Those smokers aren't enjoying the cigarette though; just the ending to the feeling of needing it. By removing that feeling, they get to feel temporarily like a non-smoker. These cigarettes are the equivalent of wearing tight shoes to get the pleasure of taking them off. So if you absolutely feel that you must have your little reward then wear a pair of tight shoes and don't take them off until you go on a break. Then you can experience the reward of relaxation and satisfaction of taking them off. Perhaps you would feel rather stupid doing this. You would be right. However, this is pretty much what smokers do all day every day. Soon you will see this whole aspect of the 'reward' for what it really is – just another occasion when smokers have to go on feeding the little monster.

If you are in a profession where you really need a break – homemakers, doctors, teachers etc., then you'll soon be enjoying that break ten times more because you can use it to really relax, not to have to ingest a battery of poisons and other harmful chemicals.

Remember, you don't need a substitute. Every pang, however minor, is a symptom of recovery and you will be fully recovered before you know it. Let that knowledge be your reward. Enjoy ridding your body of this poison and your mind of the slavery and dependence.

I have covered the topic of weight gain in Chapter 30, but weight and substitutes are so closely linked that I feel the need to reiterate the points that I have already made:

1. A nicotine pang can feel like a mild hunger pang. So if you find yourself getting 'hungry' at odd times of the day, it's more likely to be a nicotine pang. Just brush it off and celebrate yet another sign of your recovery
2. Nicotine speeds up the metabolism slightly and robs you of energy, so if you want to maintain your current weight you may need to reduce your calorific intake by a small amount. Actually, this is usually comfortably offset by the increased energy levels you feel from not having to smoke, and so many people actually lose weight if they want to on this method because instead of moping around eating chocolate and feeling deprived, you feel like getting out and doing things with all of your new-found energy and confidence

The stories we all hear about people putting twenty, thirty or forty pounds on are always due to substituting food for cigarettes. Interestingly, the medical establishment says that the average smoker could put on one hundred pounds when they quit and still be better off as a non-smoker than as a smoker. I'm not suggesting that you test this, but it does demonstrate the scale of damage and the degree of risk associated with smoking.

If there were any truth about cigarettes and weight control you would never see an overweight smoker, and there are plenty of those around; I should know, for years I was one.

Actually, if any of these myths about smoking were true, it would say so on the pack. In Canada, as in the US, there is a constitutional right to free speech. If cigarettes did in fact relieve stress, control weight, help us relax and concentrate etc., it would say it on the pack. That none of these claims appear on the pack is proof that they are not true. In fairness, it is smokers, not tobacco companies who make these claims. As a senior tobacco executive said in 1982, "We should start to see ourselves as a drug company rather than a tobacco company."

If you put on a couple of pounds over the next couple of weeks, don't worry. After years of punishment due to smoking, it takes our bodies a little while to settle back down. As I have said repeatedly; stopping smoking doesn't make you put weight on, overeating does. Be sensible, don't substitute, eat properly and exercise and you will be feeling – and looking – like a million dollars before you know it.

Chapter 38

Should I Avoid Temptation?

Up until now I have been categorical in all of my advice. The reason for this is twofold: firstly, because there are sound, practical reasons for the advice and second, because the efficacy of that advice has been proven thousands of times over by people who have quit using the EASYWAY.

On the question of whether or not to try to avoid people or situations that you associate with smoking, I regret that I cannot be categorical. Each smoker will need to decide for him or herself. I can, however, make what I hope will be helpful suggestions.

Every smoker fears that when they stop smoking they also have to stop living. I am delighted to tell you that the opposite is true – with the cigarette out of your life, you can really start living. This fear is really just a fear of the unknown and it is this that keeps us smoking year after year. There are two main components to the fear.

1. *How can I survive without the cigarette?* This is the same fear that smokers get when they are out late at night and running low on cigarettes. Of course it's caused by the cigarette. Non-smokers never feel this fear. Indeed, one of the sweetest things about becoming a non-smoker is to be free from the constant, nagging fear.

   This fear is purely psychological and thoroughly irrational. Think about it rationally. Why should we have a fear of not poisoning ourselves to death? The question should not be 'How can I survive without the cigarette?' but 'How did I survive being a smoker all these years?' It's amazing our bodies can put up with the punishment. Life without cigarettes is normal, natural and fun – look at the millions of non-smokers and ex-smokers who are getting through life quite happily without the burden of drug addiction and the slavery of smoking. They've done it and so can you. It's only smokers who obsess about cigarettes and get panicky when they can't smoke. Non-smokers couldn't care less. And neither will you once you have made the decision to break free and take your life back.

2. *Will life ever be the same without the cigarette?* This tends to be a longer-term fear. That once you are through the initial period and life becomes normal, you will be left with a void. I'm delighted to tell you that life without cigarettes is dramatically better than life as a smoker and that you will feel the benefits for the rest of your life. True, life does settle back down as you become accustomed to your freedom, energy, improved health and surplus cash, but it settles at a level way above that that a smoker has to endure. It may help to make some detailed notes about your life as a smoker. These notes can be used in the future to refer back to. Remembering how miserable life was as a smoker will help you to stay happy about getting, and staying, free. Sometimes, to appreciate our freedom, we have to remember what it was like to be a slave.

As I said, there are situations that you associate with smoking and you need to develop a strategy for dealing with them. Let's look at a couple of scenarios.

1. *'I'll keep a pack of cigarettes close by. Just in case.'* The failure rate among people that do this is several times higher than those that don't so my advice is to remove all smoking materials from your house, car, office etc. The reason for this is simple. By having cigarettes on or close to your person, you are sub-consciously positioning the cigarette as the 'solution' if you have a problem. Try to see it the way it really is. The cigarette is the problem, not the solution. Would you recommend that an alcoholic trying to quit drinking keep a bottle of scotch handy? Does a non-heroin addict carry a fix around with him 'just in case'? Shortly, you will be a non-smoker, and non-smokers don't need cigarettes.

   The worst thing about this tactic is that it creates doubt in your mind. We want to remove doubt, not create it! If you still feel the need to have cigarettes with you then I suggest you re-read this book from the beginning because something hasn't clicked.
2. *'Should I avoid stressful or social occasions?'* Try to avoid stressful situations (who needs them?) but don't be frightened of them if they do materialize. As a non-smoker you will be far better able to handle stress because you will be happier and healthier. You also won't be suffering the constant stress of being a drug addict.

As for social occasions, my view is that you have achieved something wonderful and that you should celebrate from square one, not sit at home moping. Remember – you haven't lost a friend; you've killed a deadly enemy. This enemy was not only trying to kill you, but was also stealing from you; your health, energy, self-confidence and self-esteem, money and your freedom. Why wouldn't you be happy to get rid of such an evil monster? 'Get out and enjoy yourself' is my advice. There is so much to be happy about and the sooner you get out and have fun, the sooner you receive affirmation of the wonderful decision you have made to break free.

Chapter 39

The Moment of Revelation

The moment of revelation usually takes place around three weeks after you stop. The sky appears to become brighter and as the last of the poison is finally swept away the last of the brainwashing disappears along with it. Instead of telling yourself you do not need to smoke, you suddenly realize that the last thread has been broken and you can enjoy the rest of your life without ever needing to smoke again. It is also usually from this point that you start looking at smokers as worthy of pity.

Smokers using willpower rarely experience this wonderful moment because, although they are glad to be non-smokers, they never truly understand that there was nothing to 'give up' and they continue to feel deprived.

The more you smoked, the more delightful this moment is, and the feeling lasts a lifetime.

I consider myself to have been very fortunate in this life and have had some truly wonderful moments; but the most wonderful of all was the moment of revelation. With all of the other highlights in my life I can remember how happy I was but cannot recapture the actual feeling. I just cannot get over the joy of not having to smoke any more. If ever I am feeling low and need a boost, I just think how lovely it is not to be hooked on that awful weed. Nearly all of the letters I receive from people who have broken free the EASYWAY echo this sentiment – that quitting smoking was the best thing they ever did. Ah! What pleasure you have to come!

With nearly twenty years of feedback from the clinics and the book, I have learned that most people experience the moment of revelation within days, not weeks as stated above.

In my own case, it happened even before I put out my final cigarette. This is relatively common at our clinics; a smoker will say something like "You don't have to say another word, Allen. I can see everything so clearly, I know I'll never smoke again." Over the years I have learned to tell when it happens without the individual even saying anything, and it is a thrilling moment. From the letters I receive I'm also aware that it frequently happens with the book.

Ideally, if you follow all the instructions and understand the psychology completely, it should happen to you over the next couple of days.

Nowadays at the clinic I tell smokers that the physical withdrawal period is around three days and that after three weeks you are truly free, but I dislike giving these kinds of guidelines. It can cause two problems. Firstly it creates an expectation that the smoker will have to suffer for three days or three weeks. As I have already stated, this is not so; with the right frame of mind the whole process is enjoyable right from the beginning. The second is that it creates an expectation that at the end of the third week something earth shattering will happen. As an example, it is possible that someone finds the first three weeks easy but that during the fourth, he experiences one of those dreadful days we all occasionally have, whether we're a smoker or a non-smoker. This might knock his confidence.

You might reasonably say, "Don't give any guidelines then." The problem with this is that with no expectation of what to expect, the ex-smoker is left in limbo, waiting for nothing to happen.

What is the significance of three days and three weeks? These timescales are not carved in stone but are based on the many years of feedback I've received. After three days the nicotine has left your body (as I have stated, most of it leaves in the first couple of hours) and you are technically no longer an addict. It's often around this time when the ex-smoker ceases to be pre-occupied with smoking. What usually happens is that you are in a stressful or social situation that previously you were unable to get through without smoking, and you realize that it didn't even occur to you to light up. From this point on it's usually plain sailing – don't get complacent though!

Three weeks is usually around the time when people feel that they have really broken free. This is also usually the time when most serious attempts to quit with willpower fail. Willpower quitters sense around this time that they have lost the desire to smoke and so they let their guard down. They smoke a cigarette to show themselves that they're in control and of course, get immediately re-addicted. They try not to capitulate immediately, but they are on the slippery and inexorable path back to smoking full-time.

The key to the problem is not to wait for the moment of revelation but to realize that you have total control over this process and that it is up to you to decide how you want this whole experience to play out.

If you are miserable and depressed, guess what will happen? If you are happy and excited about your new life of health, happiness and freedom, guess what will happen?

The instant you extinguish your final cigarette, it's over. You've won. No force on earth can prevent you from claiming the life that you have earned and the life you deserve. Go out, be proud, savour this moment and embrace your future free from the slavery of drug addiction.

Chapter 40

The Final Cigarette

Having decided on your timing, you are now ready to smoke your final cigarette. Before you do so, you must check two essentials:

1. Do you feel certain of success?
2. Do you have a feeling of doom and gloom or a sense of excitement and anticipation that you are on the verge of a marvelous achievement?

If you have any doubts, re-read the book first. If you still have doubts, contact your nearest Allen Carr clinic (clinic details are listed at the back of this book). One of our therapists will be happy to discuss any questions or issues you might have.

Remember, you never decided to fall into the smoking trap. But that trap is designed to enslave you for life. In order to escape you need to make the positive decision that this will be your final cigarette and that never again will you force yourself to do something that makes you feel so awful.

Remember, the only reason you have read this far is because you would dearly love to escape. So make that positive decision now. Make a solemn promise to yourself that as soon as you extinguish that final cigarette, you will never be forced to smoke another, come what may.

Perhaps you are concerned that you have made that vow to yourself in the past, but are still smoking, or that you will have to go through some dreadful trauma. Have no fear. The worst thing that can happen is that you fail, and so you have absolutely nothing to lose and so much to gain.

But why think about failure? The beautiful truth is that it is not only ridiculously easy to quit, but also extremely enjoyable. Instead, why not focus on the wonderful gifts you are about to receive as a non-smoker? Health, life, happiness, freedom...the list is endless!

Why make it hard on yourself? Why not choose the EASYWAY! All you need to do is follow the simple instructions I'm about to give you:

1. Make the solemn vow now, and mean it: I will never again do this thing that makes me so unhappy. I will never ever have to smoke another cigarette.
2. Smoke that final cigarette consciously. Inhale the filth deep into your lungs and ask yourself where the pleasure is.
3. When you extinguish it do so not with a feeling of: I must never smoke again or I can never smoke again but with the feeling: Isn't it great – I'm free! I'm no longer a slave! I don't ever have to stick one of those filthy things in my mouth again.
4. Be aware that for the next couple of days, the little monster will be inside you looking to be fed with nicotine. At times I refer to the little monster as a slight physical craving for nicotine. Strictly speaking, this is incorrect and it is important to understand why. Because it takes time for the little monster to die, some ex-smokers assume that it is necessary to suffer cravings during this period. You will be glad to know that this is not the case. The body cannot crave nicotine. Only the brain can crave. Physical withdrawal creates a slight physical feeling a bit like hunger that up to now, the brain has interpreted as 'I want a cigarette', which turns into a desire or craving to smoke. This interpretation and subsequent craving are purely mental and are merely your conditioned response to the physical stimulus, developed over years of smoking.

   You need to replace this conditioned response with a new one, based on the facts. So when that slight feeling comes, respond by saying to yourself, "YIPPEE, I'M A NON-SMOKER!" and focus on all of the wonderful gifts you are giving yourself by breaking free from the slavery of smoking. Brush that feeling off as if it were a bit of fluff that had somehow landed on your sleeve. In this way, you can be happy about your decision to become a non-smoker, and you can stay happy for the rest of your life. At this time, you can also reflect on the fact that cigarettes only ever brought misery, stress, fear and slavery to your life, and that every smoker on the planet would rather be a non-smoker.

   Willpower quitters do not recondition their 'I want a cigarette' response and therefore continue to crave cigarettes. Because they want to smoke but can't, the feeling of sacrifice and deprivation grows. This necessitates the use of willpower, which in turn leads to the feelings of panic, anxiety and stress that so many smokers associate with quitting. No wonder willpower quitters are so miserable. They spend the rest of their lives either back smoking or moping for something they hope they will never have. No wonder even the few that succeed with willpower never really feel free.

5. It is only the doubt and the waiting for nothing to happen that makes it difficult. So never doubt your decision – you know that it's the right one. We could go through the pros and cons of smoking and a thousand times out of a thousand we would choose to be a non-smoker. Having made what you know to be the right decision, don't doubt it. If you do, you put yourself in a no-win situation. You'll be miserable if you crave a cigarette but don't have one and even more miserable if you smoke it. So why bother? What would it do for you?

   Many people believe that the difference between smokers and non-smokers is the cigarette. This is only part of the story. The real difference is that non-smokers have no desire to smoke. With no desire to smoke, it takes no willpower not to do so. With no desire to smoke, there are no cravings. Why would you crave something you don't want? This is completely within your power to achieve. As soon as you make the decision, you become a non-smoker. If you are happy about your decision, you will become a happy non-smoker.

   So, you need to make the decision once and for all, and to go with that decision. Be clear in your mind that you only have two choices: you can go through the rest of your life having to smoke all day, every day, never being able to stop, living a life based on fear, misery, disease, addiction and slavery. Or you can break free, take control of your life back and build a future based on health, happiness and freedom from the slavery of smoking. The choice couldn't be easier. This isn't difficult. This is the easiest, and best, decision you'll ever make. Why not let yourself be happy! You deserve it!

YOU ARE ALREADY A HAPPY NON-SMOKER!
And you will remain one, provided:

1. You never doubt your decision.
2. You don't wait for 'something' to happen – you have already won; you're free!
3. You don't try not to think about smoking. Think about it as much as you like and every time celebrate that you have broken free.
4. You don't use substitutes – who needs a substitute for the biggest cause of preventable death in the world?
5. You see smokers for the drug addicts they are. Don't envy drug addicts – they'll be envying you. If anything, pity them.

6. Whether they are good days or bad, you don't change your life just because you have recovered from this awful disease called smoking. In fact, having recovered, you can now really start living! As the days go by and your health, both physical and mental improves, the highs will appear higher and the lows less low than when you were a smoker.
7. Whenever you think about smoking during the next few days or the rest of your life, you think: YIPPEE, I'M A NON-SMOKER!!!

Chapter 41

A Final Warning

No smoker, given the chance of going back in time to before they started smoking, would choose to become one again. Many of the smokers who consult me are convinced that if I could help them to stop, they would never dream of relapsing, yet a small percentage do fall for the same trap again.

I trust that this book will help you to find it easy to stop. But be warned: smokers who find it easy to stop can sometimes find it easy to start again because they think that it will be easy to quit again.

DO NOT FALL FOR THIS TRAP

No matter how long you have been a non-smoker or how confident you are that you could never get hooked; if you smoke again you will instantly become re-addicted.

Make it a rule of life that you don't smoke tobacco. No exceptions. Ever. Period. This is not a game. There are some things in life that you don't mess around with, and this is one of them.

If you do light a cigarette at some time in the future, what would it do for you? You would lose all of the wonderful gifts of health, happiness and freedom you have earned, and for what? So you can return to a life of fear, misery and slavery?

By making the decision to break free from smoking, you have just won life's lotto. The prize is life, happiness, health and freedom. Money cannot buy these gifts. Protect them with your life.

Chapter 42

Eighteen Years of Feedback

Since the original publication of this book I have been lucky to receive an enormous amount of feedback. Originally it was a struggle: the majority of the so-called experts criticized my method (most of them without taking the trouble to look at it in detail, I'm sad to say). Over the years, as they have seen the success of the method with their own eyes, this attitude has changed and today our most enthusiastic supporters are from the medical profession. Our clinics around the world see around 50,000 smokers every year and there are more doctors and nurses who attend than from any other field. In the UK, EASYWAY is generally considered to be the most effective quitting technique available and this reputation has spread throughout Europe where both the book and the clinics enjoy great success and a wonderful reputation.

As I write this, we are in the process of building and expanding our network of clinics in Canada and the US so that smokers in North America can also have access to the Easy Method.

I am no do-gooder. My war – which, I emphasize, is not against smokers but against the nicotine trap – I wage for the purely selfish reason that I enjoy it. Every time I hear of a smoker escaping from the prison I get a feeling of great pleasure, even when it has nothing to do with me. You can imagine the immense pleasure I obtain from the thousands of grateful letters that I have received over the years.

There has also been considerable frustration. The frustration is caused mainly by two categories of smoker. First, in spite of the warning contained in the previous chapter, I am disturbed by the number of smokers who find it easy to quit, yet get hooked again and find they can't succeed the next time. This applies not only to readers of the book but also to a few attendees at our clinics.

A man called me a few years ago. He was distraught; in fact he was crying. He said, "I'll pay you $2,500 if you can help me stop for a week. I know that if I can survive for a week, I'll be able to do it." I told him that I charged a fixed fee and that was all he needed to pay. He attended a group session and, much to his surprise, found it easy to stop. He sent me a very nice thank-you letter.

The last thing I say to smokers as they leave the clinic is: "Remember, you must never smoke another cigarette." This particular man said, "Have no fear, Allen. If I manage to stop, I'll definitely never smoke again."

I could tell that the warning hadn't really registered. I said, "I know you feel like that at the moment, but how will you feel six months on?"

He said, "Allen, I will never smoke again."

About a year later there was another phone call. "Allen, I had a small cigar at Christmas and now I'm back on forty cigarettes a day."

I said, "Do you remember when you first called me? You hated it so much that you offered me $2,500 if you could stop for a week."

"I remember. Haven't I been stupid?"

"Do you remember that you promised me that you would never smoke again?"

"I know, I've been a fool."

It's like finding someone who is up to his neck in quicksand and about to go under. You pull him out. He is grateful to you then, six months later, dives straight back in.

I admit to feeling sad, angry and frustrated at such smokers, but this quickly turns to sympathy when I realize that they are feeling ten times worse than I. If you find yourself in this situation you need to accept responsibility for your actions, give yourself an almighty kick in the pants and focus on how to clean up the mess.

If re-reading this book does not help, get a copy of ONLYWAY or contact your nearest clinic. And do it quickly.

Ironically, one of the problems with my method is that some people find it too easy. This makes them lose their fear of smoking because they figure that they can smoke when they want and find it easy to quit again. EASYWAY doesn't work that way. It is easy to stop smoking, but it's impossible to control it.

Just one cigarette led to the years of addiction and slavery you had to suffer. Just one cigarette will do it again. Do you really want to be a smoker for the rest of your life? Haven't you already decided that this is the *last* thing you want? The only thing that is essential to be a happy non-smoker is not to smoke.

The other category of smoker that causes me frustration is those smokers who are too frightened to even try or, when they do, find it a great struggle. The main difficulties appear to be the following:

1. *Fear of failure*. The point is that as a smoker, you are already a failure. You therefore have absolutely nothing to lose and potentially a tremendous amount to gain.

2. *Fear of the panic feeling and of being miserable.* These fears are caused by the cigarette. Non-smokers don't have them. One of the sweetest things about not having to smoke any more is to be free of these fears. If you begin to feel uncomfortable, slow your breathing down and take a couple of nice, big, deep breaths. Focus on the key thoughts: there is nothing to 'give up' apart from a life of fear, misery and slavery; every smoker is envious of you as a non-smoker, because every smoker would rather be a non-smoker; that the little monster is dead or already dying. If you go back to smoking you are guaranteeing a future of feeling panicky and miserable. Is that how you want to go through the rest of your life? No one can stop time. Every second that passes, the fear recedes. Enjoy your inevitable victory.

   If you want to shout, scream or cry then do so. These are all perfectly natural ways to relieve tension. Remember – you are not feeling this way because you stopped smoking, but because you started in the first place. You cannot and will not fail because your life and your future depend on your success.
3. *Not following the instructions.* Incredibly, some smokers say to me "Your method just didn't work for me." They then go on to describe how they ignored not just one instruction, but practically all of them. For clarity, I will summarize the instructions at the end of this chapter.
4. *Misunderstanding instructions.* These misunderstandings appear to be based mainly around the following:
   a. *"I can't stop thinking about smoking"* Of course you can't, and if you try to you'll create a phobia about it and this will make you miserable. It's like trying to fall asleep at night – the harder you try, the harder it becomes. It's inevitable that you will think about smoking. It's *what* you are thinking that counts. If you are thinking, "I'd love a cigarette" then you'll have to use willpower and you'll be miserable. If you are thinking how wonderful it is to be free, then you'll be happy, and the more you think about it, the happier you'll be.
   b. *"When will the little monster die?"* As I have mentioned, the nicotine leaves your body very quickly. You may continue to feel that slightly empty, insecure feeling because many other things cause it, including hunger, stress or fear – none of which are necessarily related to smoking. Incidentally, this is why so many willpower quitters never feel free – they incorrectly interpret a normal hunger pang or a slightly nervous feeling about,

say, making a presentation at work, as a nicotine pang. In any case, the feeling is so minor that most people don't even notice it. If you feel anything, brush it off and move onto something more important!

c. *Waiting for the moment of revelation.* As the saying goes: a watched kettle never boils. Don't sit around waiting for it; get out and enjoy your life and it will come. I once stopped for three weeks with willpower. I met an old school friend and ex-smoker. He asked me how I was getting on. I replied that I had survived three weeks.

   He said, "What do you mean, you've survived three weeks?"

   I said, "I've gone three weeks without a cigarette."

   He said, "What are you going to do? Survive for the rest of your life? What are you waiting for? You've done it! You're a non-smoker."

   I thought, "He's absolutely right. What am I waiting for?" Unfortunately, because I didn't understand the trap at that time, I was soon back in it, but the point was well taken. You become a non-smoker the second you extinguish your final cigarette. The important thing is to be happy from the start.

d. *"I'm still craving cigarettes."* Then you are being just plain stupid. How can you say 'I want to be a non-smoker' and then say 'I want a cigarette'? Smokers smoke; non-smokers don't. You have to decide. You already know what you want, so stop playing these ridiculous games with yourself by sabotaging this process and depriving yourself of the chance at a life of health, happiness and freedom.

e. *"When I stop smoking I stop enjoying life"* Why? All you have done is to stop poisoning and choking yourself to death. Don't be ridiculous. You have just saved your life, not lost it. Look at it this way. Over the next couple of days, you will be experiencing a very mild sensation. This sensation is so mild that most people aren't even aware of it. When you were a smoker, you experienced this sensation – a slightly empty, insecure feeling – pretty much throughout your smoking life: when you slept, when you were working, when you went to the movies etc. It didn't bother you when you were a smoker, so why let it bother you now? It didn't stop you trying to lead a full life then, so why should it do so now? Life is for living, so go out and enjoy it. If there are smokers present, so what? Remember, you are not the one being deprived; they are. Smokers are deprived of their health, their money, their self-respect, their energy, their self-esteem and their freedom. And for what do they make these incredible sacrifices? So they can remove that little empty, insecure feeling and temporarily feel like a non-smoker! Does this sound like a good deal to you? The truth is that every single one of them will be envying you. Be proud of this wonderful achievement. Enjoy your time in the spotlight! When those smokers see you so happy and comfortable, they'll think you are Superman. And, in truth, you'll feel a bit like him!

f. *"I'm miserable and irritable"* This is because you haven't followed my instructions. Find out which one it is and deal with it. Some people understand and believe everything I say but still start off with a feeling of doom and gloom, as if something terrible is happening. Of course, the truth is that something wonderful has happened. The terrible thing was when you became a smoker, and the terror continued throughout all those years of slavery. If health, happiness and freedom aren't enough for you, then you have bigger problems than smoking. Why be miserable and make it hard on yourself when the reality is that you have so much to celebrate?

THE CHECK LIST

Follow these simple instructions and you cannot fail.

1. Make a solemn vow that you will never, ever smoke, chew or suck anything that contains nicotine and stick to that vow.
2. Get this clear in your mind: there is nothing to give up. By this I don't mean that you will be better off as a non-smoker (you've known that your entire smoking life); nor do I mean that the pleasure or benefit from smoking is not worth the expense and risk. I mean that there is absolutely no benefit to smoking whatsoever, and there never was. Smoking is like banging your head against a brick wall because it feels a bit better when you stop.
3. There is no such thing as a confirmed smoker. You are just one of the millions who fell for the trap. Like millions of ex-smokers who once thought they couldn't escape, you have broken free.
4. If you were to weigh up the pros and cons of smoking, the conclusion would always be the same – to be a non-smoker and happy about it. Having made what you know to be the right decision, don't make yourself miserable by doubting it.
5. Don't try not to think about smoking or worry that you are thinking about it too much. So long as you are thinking how wonderful

it is to have broken free from the slavery of drug addiction, you'll be fine.

6. DO NOT use substitutes.
7. DO NOT keep cigarettes around.
8. DO NOT avoid smokers.
9. DO NOT change your lifestyle just because you have stopped smoking.

If you follow the above instructions, you will soon experience the moment of revelation. But:

10. Don't wait for that moment to come. Just get on with your life. Enjoy the highs and deal with the lows. The moment will come, and when it does, it's a moment of pure joy.

Chapter 43

Help the Smoker Left on the Sinking Ship

Smokers are panicking these days. There has been a huge change in society. Not too long ago, you could smoke anywhere; today smokers are shoved outside into the freezing cold. Even smokers regard smoking as anti-social. They sense that the whole thing is coming to an end, and they are right. Every year, millions of smokers are quitting and smokers left in the trap are acutely aware of this.

Every time a smoker successfully escapes from the sinking ship, the ones left on it feel more miserable and more threatened. Every smoker instinctively knows that it is ridiculous to spend a fortune for rolled up dried vegetable matter, to set light to it and to breathe the cancerous fumes into your lungs.

So smokers blatantly lie about their 'habit', not only to others, but also to themselves. They have to. This is essential if they are to retain some self-respect. They feel the need to justify what they know in their hearts to be unjustifiable behavior. They 'buy into' the brainwashing because they have no other option; and they vigorously defend their choice and their right to smoke because to admit the truth would leave them feeling frightened and stupid.

If a smoker tries to stop by using willpower, he feels deprived and miserable. All this does is to confirm to other smokers how right they are to keep smoking.

Non-smokers don't feel the need to justify their decision to be non-smokers. Some decisions are such no-brainers that they do not need explanation or justification. Smokers therefore don't really understand that it is easy and fun to be a non-smoker. Instead, they believe that becoming one will involve making a tremendous sacrifice. This intimidates the smoker and contributes to the fear that keeps him smoking.

As a non-smoker you can help smokers to see that it is easy and fun to be a non-smoker. Show the smoker that there is nothing to fear, nothing to 'give up' and absolutely everything to gain. Tell him how wonderful it is not to have to choke yourself, how lovely it is to wake up feeling fit and strong and to be able to really breathe. Tell him how great it feels to be free of the terrible, unremitting, unrewarding slavery of smoking. Tell him how it feels to finally be free of the conflict and stress of being a smoker. Even better, get him to read this book.

It is essential not to belittle the smoker by muttering away about second-hand smoke or ostentatiously waving away the smoke and pretending that it's choking you to death. Remember how much you hated such people when you were a smoker? Please don't turn into one of them, for goodness' sake. Ex-smokers already have a bad reputation with smokers. This reputation is entirely due to the influence of ex-smokers who have quit by using willpower. Part of that ex-smoker still believes that he made a sacrifice when he quit. He continues to feel somewhat vulnerable and copes with this vulnerability by attacking the smoker. This might make him feel better, but it does absolutely nothing for the smoker, apart from to confirm that all ex-smokers are miserable, sanctimonious do-gooders with nothing better to do than to tell other people how to run their lives. I had no time for such people when I was a smoker, and I have no time for them now. In this situation, the ex-smoker's attack causes the smoker to feel anxiety, frustration and fear. These add up to stress, and what's the first thing a smoker wants to do in a stress situation? That's right – light up.

Although the change in society's attitude to smoking is the main reason why so many want to quit, it doesn't make it easier for them to do so. In fact, it makes it a great deal harder.

Today in Canada every smoker who leaves his or her house is subjected to severe restrictions on where and therefore when he or she can smoke. The restrictions are so severe that the smoker becomes obsessed with planning the next opportunity to smoke. This has the effect of making every cigarette precious, and this of course feeds the illusion that there is some pleasure or functionality in smoking. The reality is that all the smoker is 'enjoying' is removing the feeling of deprivation and temporarily feeling like a non-smoker.

These periods of enforced abstinence don't even substantially reduce the amount a smoker smokes; they just mean that the smoker chain-smokes during the few occasions he or she can smoke unhindered. The smoker is 'loading up' and 'power smoking' because they don't know when their next opportunity will come around.

The tighter the smoking restrictions and the more profound the disdain society displays towards smokers, the more the smoker has to change his lifestyle to revolve around the cigarette and the more ostracized he feels.

Society has made the mistake of demonizing the victim instead of the disease. Out of the many tragedies that surround the subject of smoking, surely this is one of the most tragic.

It's strange that even though heroin addicts are technically criminals in law, our instinct as a community is to try to help them in any way we can. Let us adopt the same attitude with smokers. Smoking isn't a choice; it's an addiction. The smoker smokes because he doesn't think he can stop. The smoker endures year after exhausting year of addiction and mental and physical slavery. We always say that a quick death is better than a slow one, so do not envy the poor smoker. He deserves to be treated with sensitivity, respect and dignity. And he also deserves your pity.

Chapter 44

Advice to Non-smokers

HELP GET YOUR SMOKING FRIENDS OR RELATIVES TO READ THIS BOOK

First, study the contents of this book yourself, and try to put yourself in the place of the smoker.

Do not attempt to force him to read this book or try to stop him smoking by telling him he's ruining his health and wasting his money. He already knows this better than you do. Smokers do not smoke because they enjoy it or because they want to. They tell themselves and others this in order to retain some degree of self-respect. They smoke because they feel utterly dependent on cigarettes, because they think that the cigarette helps them to relax and cope with stress and because they sense that life cannot be enjoyable without smoking. If you try to force a smoker into quitting, this will make him want to smoke more. This makes each cigarette precious which in turn makes it harder to quit.

Instead, concentrate on the other side of the coin. Get him into the company of ex-smokers (there are more than six million of them in Canada). It will do him good to realize that there are millions of people who have been through this exact same experience. When I was a smoker it never occurred to me that all smokers felt the way I did; and that all ex-smokers had felt like this before they quit. Once he sees that there is life after quitting smoking, and that a smoke-free life is infinitely better than the half-life that smokers live, maybe he'll begin to feel a little less intimidated by the prospect of escaping.

Once you have him believing that maybe he can stop, his mind will start to open. Suggest that it seems obvious that non-smokers aren't missing out on anything, and that it looks to you like smokers don't enjoy smoking, but that they smoke to remove the need to smoke.

For many smokers, this information and observation – so obvious to non-smokers – comes as a bolt from the blue. At this stage, he is ready to start reading this book. He'll be expecting to plough through reams of statistics and technical data about lung cancer and heart disease. Tell him that this book was written by a former chain-smoker and that a grand total of nine pages of this book talk about anything related to health. Keep pointing out that it's only a book and that there is no pressure to quit – if he wants to keep smoking afterwards then he can. Tell him that one of the instructions in the book is to keep smoking – that will get his interest!

HELP DURING THE EARLY DAYS OF A QUIT

Whether an ex-smoker is suffering or not, assume that he is. Do not try to minimize his suffering by telling him how easy it is to quit. This will merely irritate him and earn you a filthy look. Instead, tell him how proud you are, how much better he looks and smells, how much easier he is breathing and point out that his smoker's cough has disappeared. Keep this praise and support going. I cannot even begin to describe how important this is.

Because he is not talking about smoking, you might think he's forgotten about it. He hasn't. Don't avoid talking about it, unless you are asked to do so.

Go out of your way to relieve him of additional stresses and pressures during the early days of his quit. Try to think of ways to make life more interesting and fun. If you want to pamper him and treat him like royalty for a while, I'm fairly sure that he won't complain.

Be aware that if the newly launched ex-smoker has a bad day, he is likely to blame it on having quit smoking. When I was trying to quit using willpower I used to throw a tantrum in the hope that my wife or friends would say "I can't bear to see you suffering like this. For goodness' sake, have a cigarette." This would thrill me because it gave me an excuse to smoke without losing face. I wasn't 'giving in'; I was being instructed to smoke. If the ex-smoker uses this ploy, under no circumstances fall for it. Instead say, "If that's what cigarettes do to you, thank goodness you'll soon be free. How wonderful it is that you had the courage and intelligence to stop."

Finale: Help End This Scandal

In my opinion, cigarette smoking is the biggest scandal in our society. I am not Canadian and it is not my place to criticize or otherwise evaluate policy developed by a Government that has been freely elected by Canadians. Indeed, it should also be noted that Canada, along with Australia, is at the forefront of the tobacco control world. However I do know that the problems with respect to tobacco control are the same the world over.

The hypocrisy is incredible. We get uptight about glue sniffing and heroin addiction, but it is smoking that is decimating our society, and it has been doing so for decades. In Canada alone, smoking kills 45,000 people every year, making it easily the biggest cause of preventable death. It is estimated that three million Canadians alive today will die from smoking related causes.

The government is by far the biggest beneficiary of tobacco sales. The most recent figures indicate that the Government takes somewhere in the region of \$8billion every year. This dwarfs even the profit that the tobacco companies make.

Each year, the Government spends around \$70m on tobacco control. This equates to less than 1% of the tax revenue generated by the sale of tobacco products. Of that miniscule \$70m, a negligible sum is spent on helping smokers quit.

The Government's annual investment in tobacco control amounts to around \$12 per smoker per year and just over \$1,500 per smoking related death. A comparable calculation for heroin reveals an annual spend of around \$454m for the estimated 170,000 users of illicit drugs excluding cannabis. This equates to around \$2,700 per user and a staggering \$908,000 per death.

There is the application of double standards here. We throw resources at heroin addicts – who are technically criminals – giving them treatment, shelter, safe injection sites and subsidized drugs or substitutes; yet the smoker – addicted through no fault of his own to a legal product – is left to suffer with little or no support and to pay a truly exorbitant price – most of which goes to the Government – to get his drug.

Doctors, who have been tasked with sticking a band-aid over this gaping wound are over-worked and poorly trained in cessation techniques. More often than not, the best a doctor can do is to say a few encouraging words and give you a prescription for a pill or patch that likely contains the drug you are trying to break free from.

In the meantime, incidence of smoking in movies, particularly in movies aimed at teenagers, has never been higher. We have legislation to make it illegal to purchase cigarettes below a certain age, but no law prohibiting possession. Schools are powerless to implement a no smoking rule, apart from in areas where smoking is banned by provincial legislation. Up until 2003 we allowed tobacco companies to continue to sponsor key sporting and cultural events and to promote their brand to impressionable children along the way. We are virtually guaranteeing that our kids will see smoking as cool, desirable and rebellious rather than sad, disgusting and depressing. In their tens of thousands, they are falling into the same trap we fell into, for the same reasons. I really cannot believe that we are standing by and letting this happen.

It is bad enough that smoking has decimated my father's, my own and, most likely, the next generation. Are we going to impose this dreadful burden onto yet another generation? Have we learned nothing?

I just don't understand it. If a salmonella or mad cow outbreak results in a single death we all but call a state of emergency; but here we have a disease which kills 125 Canadians a day (and has done for years), yet all we seem to be able to do is tax it.

In a society that spends $1 billion on a Gun Registry that is projected to save around 1,000 lives over a ten-year period, surely we can divert a similar amount to dealing with a preventable disease that kills 45,000 Canadians every single year?

It has often been said that tobacco is the only legal product that if used precisely as the manufacturer intended, kills you. How many more billions of dollars will we give tobacco companies to make products that, sadly, work too effectively? How many more innocent people are we going to let die from this terrible disease? And how many more are we going to allow to become infected with the disease in the first place?

I won't wish you luck – you don't need it. Just follow the instructions contained on the following page. Once you have broken free yourself, please spread the word. I really welcome comments and letters from readers so please feel free to contact me via your nearest EASYWAY clinic.

I wish you every success and all the best for a healthy and happy future free from the slavery of smoking.

Sincerely,
Allen Carr

Final instructions

1. Keep this book somewhere safe, in a place where you can easily refer to it. It's no bad thing to pick it up occasionally and read a couple of pages. It'll keep you 'in the zone'. Don't lose it or lend it out. This is your shortcut to attaining the right frame of mind about smoking. Keep it close at hand, in case you need it.
2. If you ever find yourself envying another smoker, remind yourself that they will be envying you. Remember that when you were a smoker, you envied non-smokers. It is not non-smokers who are being deprived; it's smokers.
3. Remember that you hated being a smoker – every smoker does. That's why you made the wonderful decision to break free. Try not to forget how miserable being a smoker made you. That way you can always be happy about not having to smoke.
4. Remember that there is no such thing as one cigarette. The first cigarette you ever smoked led to the thousands and thousands of cigarettes you were forced to smoke throughout your smoking life. If you smoke again, you will have to be a smoker all day, every day for the rest of your life.
5. Never, ever doubt your decision to break free from the slavery of smoking. You are achieving what every smoker on the planet would dearly love to achieve – freedom.
6. If you have any problems contact your nearest Allen Carr clinic. Details are listed on the following pages.

Allen Carr clinics

Hundreds of thousands of smokers have become happy non-smokers easily and permanently by attending one of Allen Carr's clinics.

Sessions are held in groups of 10-20 smokers and last around five hours. We offer all attendees a 100% money-back guarantee. For more information please call your nearest clinic or visit the appropriate website.

CANADA

Website: www.theeasywaytostopsmoking.com
Email: info@theeasywaytostopsmoking.com
Toll free: 1 866 666 4299
Seminars held in Toronto and Vancouver
Corporate programs available throughout Canada

Head Office:
P.O. Box 61051
511 Maple Grove Rd.
Oakville, ON L6J 6X0
Tel: (905) 849 7736
Fax: (905) 849 9237
Therapist: **Damian O'Hara**

USA

Website: www.theeasywaytostopsmoking.com
Email: info@theeasywaytostopsmoking.com
Toll free: 1 866 666 4299
Seminars held in New York and Los Angeles
Corporate programs available throughout the USA

Head Office:
1133 Broadway, Suite 706
New York, NY 10010
Tel: (212) 330 9194
Therapist: **Damian O'Hara**

AUSTRALIA

MELBOURNE
148 Central Road, Nunawading, 3131, Victoria.
Tel & Fax: 039894 8866.
Therapist: **Trudy Ward**.
E-mail: tw.easyway@bigpond.com

AUSTRIA

Website: www.allen-carr.at
SESSIONS ALL OVER AUSTRIA
Free line telephone for Information and Booking
0800RAUCHEN (0800 7282436)
Triesterstraße 42, Spielberg
Tel: 03512 44755 Fax: 03512 447755-14
Therapist: **Erich Kellermann and Team**
Email: info@allen-carr.at

BELGIUM

Website: www.allencarr.be

ANTWERP
Koningin Astridplein 27 B-9150 Bazel
Tel: 03 281 6255. Fax: 03 744 0608.
Therapist: **Dirk Nielandt**
E-mail: Easyway@dirknielandt.be
Therapist: **Valerie Popowski**
Tel:03 294 3065
E-mail: contact@allencarr.info
Website: www.allencarr.info

CARIBBEAN

GUADELOUPE, ANTILLES
Tel: 05 90 84 95 21
Therapist: **Fabiana de Oliveira**
E-mail: allencaraibes@wanadoo.fr

COLOMBIA, SOUTH AMERICA

BOGOTA
Cra. 9 No.77-19, Bogota
Tel: (571) 3217382
Therapists: **Felipe Calderon, Jose Manuel Duran**
E-mail: EasywayColombia@007mundo.com

DENMARK

Website: www.easyway.dk

COPENHAGEN
Asger Rygsgade 16, 1th, 1727 Copenhagen V, Denmark
Tel: 519 03536
Therapist: **Mette Fonss**
E-mail: mette@easyway.dk

ECUADOR, SOUTH AMERICA

QUITO
c/o Consulado De Austria, Gaspar de Villarroel E9-53y Av. Shyris 3er piso, Quito.
Tel & Fax: 02 2820 920
Therapist: **Ingrid Wittich**
E-mail: toisan@pi.pro.ec

FRANCE

Website: www.allencarr.fr
Central Booking Line: 0800 FUMEUR

MARSEILLE
70 Rue St Ferreol, 13006 Marseille
Tel: 04 91 33 54 55 Fax: 04 91 33 32 77
Therapist: **Erick Serre**
E-mail: allencarr@wanadoo.fr

PARIS
125 Boulevard Montparnasse– 75006 Paris
Therapist: **Erick Serre**
E-mail: allencarr@wanadoo.fr

LANGUEDOC
1051 rue de Las Sorbes, 34070 Montpellier
Therapist: **Dominique Hertogch**
E-mail: Dominique.Hertogch@wanadoo.fr

TOULOUSE
54 Avenue Crampel, 31400 Toulouse

LYON
33 rue de Bourgogne, 69009 Lyon
Therapist: **Michel Guyot**

ALSACE
48 rue des Vignes, 67202 Wolfisheim
Therapist: **Emanuel Klein**

COTE D'AZUR
Porte de l'arenes hall C, 455 Promenade des anglais,
06299 Nice Cedex 3
Therapist: **Elaine Mahon**

GERMANY

Website: www.allen-carr.de
E-mail: info@allen-carr.de
SESSIONS ALL OVER GERMANY
Free line telephone for information and central booking line:
08000RAUCHEN (0800 07282436)
Kirchenweg 41, D-83026 Rosenheim
Tel: 8031 463067 Fax: 8031 463068
Therapists: **Erich Kellermann and Team**

ICELAND

REYKJAVIK
Skeidarvogur 147, 104 Reykjavik
Tel: 553 9590 Fax: 588 7060
Therapists: **Petur Einarsson & Valgeir Skagfjord**
E-mail: easyway@easyway.is

REPUBLIC OF IRELAND

DUBLIN
44 Beverly Heights, Knocklyon, Dublin 16
Lo-Call (From ROI) 1 890 ESYWAY (379929)
Tel: 01 494 1644 (4 lines) Fax: 01 495 2757
Therapist: **Brenda Sweeney**
E-mail: info@allen-carr.ie

CONNAUGHT
Tel and Fax: 094 67925
Therapist: **Pat Melody Dunnc**

ITALY

Website: www.easywayitalia.com

MILAN
Via Dante 76, 20092 Cinisello Balsamo, Milan
Tel: 02 6129 3843
Mobile: 0348 354 7774
Therapist: **Francesca Cesati**
E-mail: info@easywayitalia.com

NETHERLANDS

Website: www.allencarr.nl

AMSTERDAM
Pythagorasstraat 22, 1098 GC Amsterdam.
Tel: 020 465 4665 Fax: 020 465 6682
Therapist: **Eveline de Mooij**
E-mail: amsterdam@allencarr.nl

UTRECHT
De Beaufortlaan 22B, 3768 MJ Soestduinen (gem. Soest).
Tel: 035 602 94 58
Therapist: **Paula Rooduijn**
E-mail: soest@allencarr.nl

ROTTERDAM
Mathenesserlaan 290, 3021 HV Rotterdam.
Tel: 010 244 0709 Fax: 010 244 07 10
Therapist: **Kitty van't Hof**
E-mail: rotterdam@allencarr.nl

NIJMEGEN
Van Heutszstraat 38, 6521 CX Nijmegen
Tel: 024 336 03305
Therapist: **Jacqueline van den Bosch**
E-mail: nijmegen@allencarr.nl

NEW ZEALAND

AUCKLAND
472 Blockhouse Bay Road, Auckland 1007
Tel: 09 6265390 Mobile: 027 4177077
Therapist: **Vickie Macrae**
E-mail: ezywaynz@hotmail.com
Website: www.easywaynz.nz

NORWAY

Website: www.easyway-norge.no

OSLO
Munkedamsveien. 53b 0250 Oslo
Tel: 22 83 21 00 Fax: 23 2728 15
Therapist: Dag Hognerud
E-mail: post@easyway-norge.no

PORTUGAL

OPORTO
Rua dos Castanheiros, 97
4455-089 Lavra – Matosinhos
Tel: 22 9958698
Therapist: **Ria Monteiro**
E-mail: slofmont@mail.telepac.pt

SOUTH AFRICA

Website: www.allencarr.co.za
Central Booking Line: 0861 100 200

CAPETOWN
15 Draper Sq. Draper St, Claremont 7708
Tel: 0861 100 200 Fax: 021 852 2014
Therapist: **Dr. Charles Nel**
E-mail: easyway@allencarr.co.za

PRETORIA
Therapist: **Dudley Garner**
Tel: 0861 100 200
E-mail: info@allencarr.co.za

SPAIN

Website: www.comodejardefumar.com

MADRID and BARCELONA – (other areas also available)
Tel: 902 10 28 10 Fax: 942 83 25 84
Therapists: **Geoffrey Molloy & Rhea Sivi and Team**
E-mail: easyway@comodejardefumar.com

SWITZERLAND

Website: www.allen-carr.ch
Free line telephone for Information and Booking:
0800RAUCHEN (0800 7282426)
Schontalstrasse 30, Ch - 8486 Zurich-Rikon.
Tel: 52 3833773 Fax: 52 3833774
Therapist: **Cyrill Argast and Team**
E-mail: info@allen-carr.ch

UK

Website: www.allencarrseasyway.com

LONDON
lc Amity Grove, Raynes Park, London SW20 OLQ
Tel: 020 8944 7761 Fax: 020 8944 8619
Therapists: **John Dicey, Sue Bolshaw, Colleen Dwyer, Crispin Hay, Jenny Rutherford**
E-mail: postmaster@allencarr.demon.co.uk

BIRMINGHAM
415 Hagley Road West, Quinton, Birmingham B32 2AD.
Tel & Fax: 0121 423 1227.
Therapists: **John Dicey, Colleen Dwyer, Crispin Hay**
E-mail: postmaster@allencarr.demon.co.uk

BOURNEMOUTH & SOUTHAMPTON
Tel & Fax: 01425 272757
Therapist: **John Dicey, Colleen Dwyer**

BRISTOL & SWINDON
Tel: 0117 950 1441
Therapist: **Charles Holdsworth Hunt**
E-mail: stopsmoking@easywaybristol.co.uk
Website: www.easywaybristol.co.uk

BRIGHTON
Tel: 01425 272757
Therapists: **John Dicey,Colleen Dwyer**

EXETER
Tel: 0117 950 1441
Therapist: **Charles Holdsworth-Hunt**
E-mail:stopsmoking@easywayexeter.co.uk
Website: www.easywayexeter.co.uk

KENT
Tel: 01622 832 554
Therapist: **Angela Jouanneau**
E-mail: easywaykent@yahoo.co.uk

MANCHESTER
Freephone: 0800 804 6796
Therapist: **Rob Groves**
E-mail: stopsmoking@easywaymanchester.co.uk
Website: www.easywaymanchester.co.uk
Therapist: **Eva Gray (Weight)**

NORTH EAST
10 Dale Terrace, Dalton-le-Dale, Seaham,
County Durham, SR7 8QP.
Tel/Fax: 0191 581 0449.
Therapist: **Tony Attrill**

READING
Tel: 014245 272757
Therapist: **John Dicey, Colleen Dwyer**

SCOTLAND
Sessions held throughout Scotland
Tel: 0131 228 5893
Therapist: **Joe Bergin**
E-mail: bergin@napieruni.fsnet.co.uk
Website: www.easywaytostop.co.uk

SOUTH WALES
Cardiff
Tel: 0117 950 1441
Therapist: **Charles Holdsworth-Hunt**
E-mail: stopsmoking@easywaycardiff.co.uk
Website: www.easywaycardiff.co.uk

YORKSHIRE
Freephone: 0800 804 6796
Therapist: **Rob Goves**

Discount voucher for Canadian & US Allen Carr clinics

Receive a discount to the value of the price of this book when you attend any of Allen Carr's Canadian or US clinics.

Allen Carr has a network of clinics across the North American continent where he guarantees that you will find it easy to stop smoking or a full refund of your fee.

The success rate based on this money back guarantee is over 90%.

When you arrive at your session present this voucher and you will receive a discount off our fee equivalent to the price of this book. Please contact your nearest clinic for more information on how the sessions work and to book your appointment.

Some happy readers...

After being a smoker for 20 years, I was very skeptical that a book could ever help me to stop the nasty habit. As I finished the final page I put out my final cigarette and I have never had another!! That was almost six years ago. Buying this book was the best money I ever spent.

Sharon from Thunder Bay, ON

Anyone who is interested in quitting smoking should definitely read this amazing book. Not sure if the technique is simply suggestive thinking or what - but he helped both my mother and myself quit smoking permanently.

Jennie Smith, Surrey, BC

This book is absolutely amazing. It was recommended to me by the cashier at my local supermarket. It worked for her and 2 people she knew. I tried it and it was so easy. I smoked for 15 years, nothing ever worked, I was horrible to be around when I tried to quit, but not this time! Everyone at home and at work was amazed at how easily I quit. Also I did not gain any weight when I quit, which is a definite bonus.

Melissa, Vancouver, BC

This book was recommended by an acquaintance during a party. It sounded mystical and people would mysteriously quit smoking after reading. I was skeptical. Well, I bought it and read it over the weekend. By Monday, I had quit smoking. Carr does not employ scare tactics about health concerns or tries to convert you because smoking is bad for you. He simply presents you the alternative lifestyle that smokers have chosen with that of non-smokers and what you are missing on. Instead of trying to quit smoking, you find yourself trying to gain freedom. I have tried many times before through many means but this book permits you to do it without pills, patches or gimmicks.

Louis Rouillard, Kingston, ON

I read this book over the span of a week. I actually quit before finishing the book because of the way it points out how stupid smoking is in the first place. I have no cravings for cigarettes at all any more and I just ordered 2 more copies for friends and family. We've circulated this book through a group of friends of ours. So far 8 people have read it. All 8 have quit smoking. How's that for statistics?

Paul, Burnaby, BC

I quit smoking after reading Allen Carr's book. I am 51 years old and have been smoking for 36 years. I didn't think it would be possible for me to quit ... I don't like to deprive myself. But (I know this sounds unbelievable), it was easy to quit after reading this book.

David, Ottawa, ON

I smoked for 21 years and had tried to quit over a dozen times. It took me a day and half to read the book. When I started to read I KNEW that it wasn't going to work. When I finished the book I never had another cigarette. It's been 2 years now and I'm as certain as I was the day I finished reading the book that I'll never again have another cigarette. I've also loaned the book to several friends and family and every one of them who has read it has also quit. I recommend it to anyone who is currently struggling and also to those non-smokers out there who are still under the impression that they are missing out on something by not smoking.

Lori Wenger, Red Deer, AB

It is hard to believe that a book could stop me smoking - without an ounce of worry, or yearning for a cigarette. I am 25, and had been smoking about a pack a day for 11 years. I know about 5 people who have quit with this book - it is totally amazing - and no guilt tactics either! Best money I ever spent...

Chris, Vancouver, BC

The title of the book is Easy way to stop smoking and it really is. I smoked for 10 years and by reading this book it changed the way I looked at smoking. If you smoke and want to quit (we all do) read it, it works.

Bill, Brampton, ON

I read this book and was a non-smoker before I extinguished my last cigarette! It's hard to explain but it actually works.

Heather Bell, Toronto, ON

I smoked for 15 years and there was no way I could quit, read the book and it WAS EASY! No deprivation, no substitutes, just quit! I've bought 18 copies for my friends, they all smoke. Read the book, you will quit, it's that easy.

Justin, Calgary, AB

A friend lent me the book to read and I believe that it has changed my whole way of thinking. Instead of feeling deprived I feel enlightened. Everyone who ever thought it impossible to quit smoking should read this book.

Jill Sheffield, Nepean, ON

4 people out of my family read the book and we have all quit for good. The book is simple but it works. I've been a non-smoker for over 2 years now and I seriously don't miss it.

Nathalie Rivard, Mississauga, ON

This book is great! It rationalizes all the misconceptions about smoking and I would recommend this book to anyone - including non-smokers who want to understand why smokers get hooked. Buy this for your friend/family member who smokes. Unlike most other quitting books, this one asks that you smoke until he asks you to have your final cigarette....followed by no nic fits!

Erin Roths, Toronto, ON

I had been a heavy smoker for 20 years who had tried all of the conventional available methods-gum, patches, zyban - the works - all with no success. Read the book and have been free now for seven weeks. Entirely different approach and makes you realize that you are truly not giving anything up when you quit and to the contrary will experience incredible gains.

Tony Mayall, Edmonton, AB

This book is amazing. I read it and I quit, I gave it to my wife and she quit. We gave it to our friend and he quit, who then gave it to his brother and he quit. You get the idea. This book is an incredible find. Do you want to quit smoking or know someone who does? Then forget about patches, gum, hypnosis, acupuncture, or even willpower! All you need is the material in this book and you can be free from tobacco (in any form) quickly and easily.

Nate King, New Westminster, BC

I was skeptical and psychologically unready, believing I 'enjoyed' smoking and couldn't live without it...I bit the bullet and read the book, gave up immediately and haven't smoked since, it's been 6 months and I am confident I never will again. I smoked for 22 years and had tried many times with many ways but this one actually worked, so go on...change your life for the better!!!

Caroline Lloyd, Barrie, ON

This book will stop you from smoking and you will never feel like smoking again. I went from 30 a day to zilch without any cravings. Don't worry about how dependent you think you are on butts, read this book and give up with very little effort.

David Burns, North York, ON

I read this book a year ago whilst on holiday in Europe and stopped smoking. I went from 20 a day to being a really happy and relieved non-smoker, and a year down the line am 100% sure that I will never touch a cigarette again - the best thing is that I don't miss them in the slightest and what's more it doesn't even bother me whether people smoke around me or not. This is without a doubt the most wonderful book I have ever read.

Patricia Wilson, Peterborough, ON

Being a complete cynic, I did not believe for one minute that this book would work where patches and willpower had failed me. I smoked 25 to 30 a day for ten years before I read this book. I have not had a cigarette since, and I have not had the mood swings or the nervousness that I had previously suffered. The book is straight talking, easy to follow, and really does work. I would recommend this method to anyone!

Julie Brady, Edmonton, AB

Like most smokers I have "given up" hundreds of times! Not only will this book stop you smoking for good it will explain why you didn't stop completely before. I feel that my life has changed and I will NEVER smoke again. I cannot recommend this book highly enough. I have already bought copies for three of my friends! It should be available from Health Canada.

Rick Boxall, Calgary, AB

I haven't had a cigarette for three months. I have no cravings and I am sure that I will never smoke again. From someone who was a 20 a day smoker for 13 years, these are words that I never thought I'd hear myself saying. Buy the book. It works.

Maggie Newbold. London, ON

This book has worked for me (over 2 years on the wagon, now) and for several friends. Could not tell you why. No one ever can. The most important thing about Carr's approach is that it does not simply stop you smoking - it stops you wanting to smoke at all. When you think of the tremendous success rate - possibly one of the most important written works of the last 20 years.

Tim Sanderson, Victoria, BC

If you want to give up smoking, you HAVE to read this book. I smoked my last cigarette before I had even finished reading it and I know I will never smoke again. I can't believe how amazing I feel! I went from a 20 a day habit over 15 years to being a completely happy non-smoker. I wake up happier and happier about it every day - you can do it too! I work full time in a pub and live with smokers, and I STILL don't want to smoke any more. I feel as if I have been cured of a terrible disease.

Charles Cooper, Toronto, ON

Enjoy smoking? Helps you relax? Helps you concentrate? Just like a cigarette with a pint? Only smoke a couple a day? Think AGAIN......I've lent this book to eight people. Now I know 8 ex-smokers. Please read this book.

Kirk Roubillard, Ottawa. ON

When I posted this review on Amazon there were 201 reviews of which 4 people said that it didn't work for them. ALL the rest gave it 5 stars and said it was a miracle! I stopped by using this book nearly 3 years a go and I know I will never go back to being a smoker. Despite relationship breakups, redundancy etc. still no butts. This book changed my life.

James Jordan Watson, Kingston, ON

NOTES

NOTES

NOTES

NOTES